BOAT REPAIR
MADE
EASY

ENGINES

JOHN P. KAUFMAN

Editor: E. Robert "Bob" Lollo

BRISTOL FASHION PUBLICATIONS, INC.
Enola, Pennsylvania

Published by Bristol Fashion Publications, Inc.

Library of Congress Catalog Card Number: 96-85908

ISBN: 1-892216-03-5

Contribution acknowledgments

Cover Photo: Caterpillar Inc.
Inside Graphics: As Noted.

Dedication

To Uncle Tom, who instilled his love of boats in me.
To Uncle Virgil, who always had time to take me fishing.
To Pap, who took me to the river and to Nan who let him.
To Mom and Dad, who stood by me, come what may.
To John and Wendy Beeson, who helped me start this project
in Beaufort, South Carolina.
To Bob and Karen Lollo, I never would have written any
book, if not for these two great people.
To Marvin McCord, who kept pushing me to write.
To Phil and Deb Brillon, who knew when I needed a break.
To Will, who gave great engine advice and information.
To my all friends and fellow boaters, for their help and input.

INTRODUCTION

I would like to take this opportunity to welcome you to the boating family. Many of us have been around boats all of ours lives. Still many are new to the pleasures of boat ownership and the joy it can bring to all involved. I will, over the course of this book, endeavor to help all of you, regardless of your talents or experience.

The heart of any boat is her engine. The engine and its related support systems must be maintained to high standards if your boat is to be safe, reliable and a pleasure to board. Certain jobs must be accomplished on a regular schedule if you expect your boat to operate to your satisfaction.

We are about to embark on projects that will save you money on your boat work. The projects will be handled in a step-by-step method of explanation. The tools needed will be referred to as warranted, as will product names. If I have used a product or tool with great success it will be mentioned and you can use it with confidence. The projects in this book can be accomplished by most novice handy persons. I am not writing to the 20 year professional. They don't need my books, although many do buy them. If you are more experienced in your craftsmanship skills you will find this book will reinforce what you have learned and possibly show you a new method of doing an old job. Many of these will save time and most will save money in one way or another.

The projects will cover most everything you will need to know to keep your vessel in good, safe, working order with a minimum of time and money spent.

I hope your life on the water will be as enjoyable as mine has been, for you will soon find there is no better way to spend a day, a week, or a lifetime than simply "Messing About On Boats".

John P. Kaufman

TABLE OF CONTENTS

CHAPTER ONE

DIESEL ENGINES

The heart of any boat is its power plant, whether this is a small outboard on the ship's tender, or a massive reactor aboard a modern naval vessel. Regardless of size, type, intended use or the size of the vessel it is propelling through the water, the engine is top dog aboard the boat.

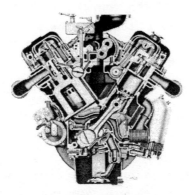

Courtesy of Detroit Diesel

Standard V type diesel engine.

After the demise of steam power, diesel engines where once the most common, if not the only, means of propulsion machinery available for large naval vessels. With the advent of nuclear propulsion systems, this is no longer the case. The days of walking into the engine room, aboard a naval vessel, and marveling at the massive components of the enormous diesel engines are all but gone. In their place are the sparkling high-tech components of the new systems. So much for fond memories.

Modern diesel engines are available from six horse-power to over fifteen hundred horsepower. They are capable of running permanent and portable gensets, auxiliary engines for sail boats, main engines for power boats and even outboards for day boats, of any description.

Diesel engines remain the work horse of most sailing vessels and motoryachts, over twenty-five feet. This has come about for extremely good reasons. The main one being, naturally aspirated diesel engines seem to run forever, with only routine maintenance, fuel and air. Herein lies the key to diesel engine longevity.

Many people run their boats as they do their cars. They get behind the wheel, turn the key and go! When the car begins its early demise, from lack of maintenance, the mechanic or new car salesman becomes rich. The owner, significantly poorer. This does not have to be, but it is an all too common mind set of boaters.

There are many safety and economic concerns with this type of thinking. When a car breaks down, you pull off to the side of the roadway and call for a seventy-five dollar tow. On the water, the breakdown will only happen in an area where there is no place to "pull over". Not to mention, the tow will cost a minimum of two hundred and fifty dollars. In short, your boat is not your car, it is your boat. It requires a more disciplined maintenance schedule, if this scenario is to be avoided.

In the most simplistic of terms, a diesel engine requires only two ingredients to function: Air and Fuel. Unlike its gasoline counter part, once a diesel engine is running it does not need electricity to maintain the spark which ignites the fuel.

Its basic function requires the correct ratio of atomized fuel and air. This mixture is compressed, at the top of the cylinder, by the piston's up stoke. When the explosive level is reached, combustion takes place, which in turn drives the piston down, providing power. Simple, isn't it?

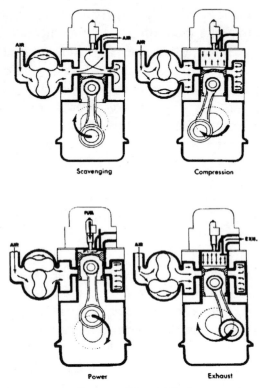

Courtesy of Detroit Diesel

The four phases (Scavenging, Compression, Power, Exhaust) of combustion for a two cycle diesel engine.

This basic function, however, requires that every part of the engine is operating at peak performance. Higher horse-power, non-naturally aspirated engines, (turbo charged, inter or after cooled engines) insist on this peak performance each time the key is turned. The naturally aspirated engines will operate a short time, although poorly, without peak performance of all the components.

I mention this, not to lull you into thinking the naturally aspirated diesel does not need the same vigilance of the turbo diesel, it does. I mention it to abolish the old adage "If it ain't broke don't fix it." Many people still believe this to be true. Their engine may be spewing oil and fuel from every conceivable orifice, missing on two of four cylinders, blowing more smoke than a fog machine and putting an oil slick on the water for miles. But it still runs, so it ain't broke. Yes, it is!

A turbo charged diesel would have shut down long before it reached this stage, possibly protecting the engine from severe damage. The naturally aspirated engine may not. Herein lies the problem of the above thinking. This lack of maintenance and concern will result in irreversible damage to the engine. I am a firm believer in repairing a problem before it is a problem. Preventive maintenance.

I am certain, the above has cleared any thoughts of further procrastination.

Considering the engine is the heart, the oil is its life's blood. Without the proper amount, weight and type of oil, the engine is doomed. The owner's manual for your engine will give you the recommended viscosity, type and oil change intervals in hours. Adhere to these recommendations above all else.

Regardless of the hours on the engine, the oil must be changed at least every six months. Oil will break down over a six month period and loose a great deal of its lubricating ability. During winter storage a stabilizer may be added to maintain the oil's integrity. Decommissioning an engine is discussed in detail in this book's companion, *Boat Repair Made Easy -- Haul Out*.

An oil change is not difficult to perform but it can be messy, if you are not diligent with details. There are a few items which will make the job considerable easier.

A filter wrench is necessary, if you have spin on filters.

A hose running from the oil pan drain plug to a point well above the oil pan, should be installed if one is not present on the engine. This is accomplished, after the oil has been drained from the engine. The new hose will not help with this oil change, but future oil changes will be less stressful.

Remove the oil pan plug and install a barbed fitting, with matching thread size, in the hole. The barbed end should accept a minimum of a 3/8" ID reinforced rubber hose. Double clamp the hose to the fitting.

The opposite end of the hose must be lead to a point above the top of the oil pan and secured with a retaining strap or clamp. A barbed fitting, with female threads and a pipe plug, must be double clamped in this end of the hose. When this hose is used to change the oil, the pipe plug is removed and an adapter threaded in place to accept the oil change pump hose.

This simple improvement will allow the oil to be pumped out of the engine and directly into a bucket for disposal. It eliminates the need to drain the oil into a container and then into the bucket for disposal.

There are many oil change pumps marketed with a 12 VDC pump mounted on a bucket. The inlet hose is run from the oil pan's pick up tube and the discharge hose drains into the bucket. They work well, but take up a good deal of storage room and they are expensive.

Many manufacturers produce a hand pump with a tube which is inserted into the dipstick tube. The oil is pumped out of the pan through the pump and into a bucket. This type of pump will rarely remove all the oil in the pan. The pick up tube of the pump, if inserted too far or not far enough, will generally miss the oil in the bottom of the pan.

I prefer a simple electric drill pump, by Jabsco. This unit is attached to a drill with the hoses being run in the same manner as the 12 VDC pump. When the oil change is complete, the pump stores in a zip lock bag, taking little space. This pump cost about twenty dollars.

If you believe your engine is contaminated with sludge from prior improper maintenance, the following process will help remove the sludge. Before warming the engine, add one quart of kerosene to the crankcase for every five quarts of engine oil, but never more than two quarts. Warm the engine to one half the normal running temperature, but not longer than ten minutes. Shut down the engine and change the oil as described below. Engines with an oil capacity of more than five quarts, should have an equal amount of oil drained before the kerosene is added. As an example, a ten quart system should have two quarts of oil drained, before adding the two quarts of kerosene.

The first step for any oil change is warming the engine to one half operating temperature. Shut down the engine and allow the oil to drain back into the pan, for a minimum of thirty minutes. Remove the oil filler cap. The oil can now be drained from the pan using one of the methods discussed above.

Remove the oil filter with a filter wrench, if it is a spin on design, and discard the filter. If the filter is a canister type, the element is inside a steel canister. Loosen the canister and drain as much oil as possible, before removing the canister entirely. The canister may have a drain plug to facilitate draining.

A spin on filter is replaced by "spinning" it onto the mounting stud. Before the filter is installed, the rubber gasket must have a thin film of oil applied to it. This step will prevent leaks and allow the filter to be easily removed at the next oil change. Turn the filter onto the stud, until the gasket makes contact with the base. After contacting the base, the filter must be turned an additional one half to two thirds of a turn, (as stated on the filter) to provide the correct seal. Turning it further will make it difficult to remove and turning it less will allow it to leak.

After removing the canister type filter, remove the

element from the canister and discard it properly. Clean the canister well, using a parts brush and diesel fuel or parts cleaner. Dry the inside and insert the new element. The rubber or fiber gasket, located where the rim of the canister contacts the base, must be replaced. This can be removed by prying it out of the base, using a blunt tipped tool. Apply a film of oil to the new gasket and install the gasket.

Hold the canister in place with the stud protruding from the top of the canister. Start the threads of the stud before positioning the canister itself. Caution must be used, to prevent cross-threading the stud. Turn the stud until the canister has made contact with the gasket. Be certain to check the alignment of the canister to the base and snugly tighten the stud, but do not over tighten.

Some engine design engineers, I am certain, take great pleasure in locating an inverted filter in an out of the way location. If this is the case with your engine, the best to hope for is catching most of the oil and cleaning the drip pan thoroughly, after the spill. There are remote oil filter location kits available which allows the oil filter to be moved to a more convenient location.

The next step is adding the correct amount of the proper viscosity and type of oil, to the crankcase. Do not over fill the engine. I suggest using all but the last two quarts required. Then allow thirty minutes for the oil to drain into the pan. Check the oil level on the dipstick and add more oil if indicated.

The final step is checking for leaks. Start the engine and allow the oil pressure to build. Check the oil filter, oil pan drain and fill cap for signs of leaks. If there are leaks tighten the offending component, wipe the oil clean and check again. When all is leak free the engine can be shut down. Wait thirty minutes and check the engine oil level. It is not uncommon for the engine to require more oil after the initial run.

Consider adding a product, such as Slick 50, during the oil change. This product significantly reduces wear at start-up and during long periods of slow idle, when oil pressure is low.

Changing a fuel filter is accomplished using the identical steps, outlined above, for the two types of oil filters, with these two exceptions. The gasket must be coated with a thin film of fuel oil, not motor oil. The filter must also be filled with fuel before its final installation. Failure to fill the filter with fuel may result in an air trap, which can only be removed by bleeding the engine's fuel system.

The first step for a complete tune up will be the purchase of a shop manual for your engine. Many after-market companies print these manuals to include most of the repairs you will need to accomplish on your engine. They also include valuable information such as capacities, torque settings, filter types and tune up specs to name a few. I do not know a single mechanic that does not own one of these books for each type of engine they repair.

A few steps should be taken to assure a professional quality job, both in performance and appearance.

A clean engine has many advantages. It is easier to work on, easier to spot fluid leaks, it will run cooler and will appear professionally maintained. Still many people believe this simple step to be a waste of time. I do not agree in the least.

While the engine is still warm from the oil change, use an engine cleaning product to remove all the grease, grime, and general crust from the outside of the engine. Be certain the air intake is well covered before you apply this product to the engine. Follow the manufacturer's directions for the application and removal of the product you have chosen.

I do not suggest products which require the use of a hose to wash off the product and the dirt it has removed. If you do choose one of these, turn off all DC and unplug the AC power cord. Use *extreme caution* when spraying a hose in the engine room. You do not want water on wiring, electronic or electrical equipment.

After the engine has been cleaned and has had time to cool down you can start the adjustments to the different components. I have a routine I use for every engine I tune. I stay with this routine time and time again. In doing so I find I do not forget any of the necessary steps. I recommend you follow the procedures as outlined in your engine's shop manual. By doing so you will not leave any procedure unattended.

Diesel engines vary greatly in their design between the different manufacturers. I will not attempt to explain the tune up or adjustment procedures for diesel engines, in this book. I, will again, strongly suggest purchasing a shop manual for your specific engine and follow the stated procedures to the letter. Do not overlook or fail to complete any part of the tune-up procedures, stated in the manual. Many of the adjustments rely on the condition that other adjustments have been completed.

The shop manual may state a particular tool is needed for an adjustment. If the manual states a part number for this tool, chances are good it can only be purchased through an authorized parts center. These specialized tools are often manufactured to extremely close tolerances, which is reflected in the cost. It is tempting to fabricate your own makeshift tool, but it may not work as intended.

One maintenance chore which is often over looked is checking the condition of the coolant. The antifreeze/coolant must be checked, each season, to be certain it has not lost effectiveness. This product, as with oil and fuel, breaks down after a certain amount of time and needs to be replaced to remain effective.

To check the effectiveness of the antifreeze, purchase an antifreeze tester from any automotive or discount store. This tool cost about two dollars. The instructions are simple, as is the tools itself. The following process should be used, if the tester indicates the antifreeze needs replaced.

Remove the heat exchanger cap or expansion tank cap

to view the antifreeze. Start the engine. Run the engine until you can see the fluid flowing in the heat exchanger or expansion tank. Add a flushing treatment, if needed, following the manufacturer's directions for its use. This product is only needed if the engine is running hot, or there is poor circulation in the heat exchanger.

CAUTION: The coolant you are about to drain will be extremely hot!

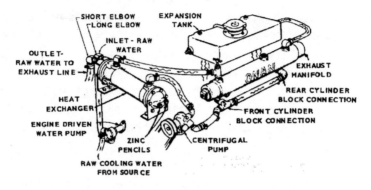

Courtesy of Onan

Fresh water cooling system which contains the coolant. System components will vary in size and shape as the engine's horsepower increases but the related system parts are basically the same.

Shut down the engine and drain the entire contents of the system, including the block. Most engines have drain cocks to facilitate draining the block. If they are frozen shut or nonexistent, try disconnecting hoses to further drain the system. Close the drain cocks and connect the hoses. If a flushing treatment was used, fill the system with water only. Warm the engine, with the heat exchanger cap removed, and drain the system again.

Fill the system with the recommended mixture of antifreeze and water as stated on the antifreeze bottle or in your owner's manual. Start the engine and check for leaks, while keeping a close eye on the coolant level. Top off the coolant and replace the cap.

When you have accomplished all the above procedures and the procedures listed in the shop manual, you can consider the routine maintenance of your engine complete and of a professional quality.

There are several common problems associated with diesel engines. I will discuss some of these problems along with the procedures used for trouble shooting or repair. Fuel, fuel filters and problems derived from clogged filters, bad fuel or contaminated tanks are discussed in Chapter Three, *Fuel Supply Systems*.

The most common problem plaguing the diesel engine is bad fuel. This results in clogged injectors or water in the system. An obstructed injector will not supply the correct amount of fuel to the cylinder which will cause a misfire in that cylinder. The result is a rough running, inefficient engine. If not attended to, in short order, this can cause other damage to the engine.

If the engine begins to run rough, similar to a gasoline engine with a fouled spark plug, the injectors must be removed and checked by a qualified technician.

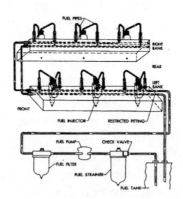

Courtesy of Detroit Diesel

Engine fuel system for a V-block engine.

You can isolate the clogged or weak injector, on most engines, by using the following procedure. However, if one injector is clogged or weak, the others may soon require servicing as well. I believe this check should only be used to limit the problem's scope to an injector fault and not another problem, disguised as a faulty injector. If the misfiring is found to be a faulty injector it is better to remove all the injectors for servicing or replacement.

There are two basic types of injector mountings. One type utilizes threads on the exterior of the injector body and matching threads in the cylinder head. The injector is threaded into the head and tightened to a specific torque setting, as stated in your shop manual. This will require the use of a torque wrench with the correct size socket and possibly, a specialized adapter.

The second type requires the use of a retaining clamp which is held in place with one or more bolts. The injector is placed in the head and the retainer clamp is placed over the top of the injector. The bolt(s) can be threaded in place and tighten, with a torque wrench, to the specific torque settings, as stated in the shop manual.

Determining which injector is at fault, is accomplished by restricting the fuel flowing to the injectors, one at a time. The first step is to gain access to the injectors. Many engines have the injectors mounted on the exterior of the engine. Others have the injectors under the rocker arm (valve) cover. If the latter is the case, the covers must be removed to gain access to the injectors. When the covers are replaced, be certain to use a gasket sealing compound, such as Permatex®, to help prevent oil leaks.

Each injector has a fuel supply and a fuel return line. The supply line is the line leading from the injector pump which is feed by the fuel filters. The supply line is the only line to be dealt with, for this procedure. Fuel filters are discussed in Chapter Three, *Fuel Supply Systems*.

I always start at the front of the engine and work

towards the rear of the engine. In this manner, I do not forget to check any of the injectors.

The injectors should now be exposed and the engine running at idle. Use the proper size wrench to slightly loosen the fuel supply line to the forward most injector. A slight amount of fuel should run from the fuel line fitting (Prevent this fuel from running into the engine by using a clean rag held under the fitting. Use caution to prevent the rag from entanglement in the moving components.) and the engine's misfiring should intensify. If the engine's misfiring does not intensify, tighten the fitting and move on to the next injector, repeating the same procedure. If the engine still does not misfire the fittings are not being loosen sufficiently or both injectors are faulty. To ascertain which is the cause, tighten this fitting and start over with the first injector. If the first injector still does not misfire this may be the clogged injector. Tighten the fitting and continue with testing the balance of the injectors, using the same procedures. Note any injectors which do not cause the misfiring to intensify. These injectors must be remove and serviced or replaced with new injectors, using the steps outlined in your shop manual.

The principle behind this test is simple. By loosening the fuel supply line to the injector, the flow of fuel to the injector, and therefore the cylinder, has been decreased. This decreased flow imitates a clogged injector, thus forcing that cylinder to misfire. If the engine's misfiring does not intensify when the injector's fuel supply line is loosened, that injector can be suspected as the cause of the misfiring engine.

Faulty injectors will not only cause the engine to misfire but can also cause excessive smoke to emanate from the exhaust. Another frequent cause of this smoking condition, is a clogged air box drain. To check the air box drain, start the engine and allow it to idle. If the drain is equipped with a check valve, the engine must be at operating temperature before the check valve will open. This will then allow air to flow from the drain tube. If there is no check valve in place, the air will flow as soon as the engine is started.

To check the air flow, place your finger over the end of the drain tube. If you can not feel a constant flow of air from the tube, the tube or valve is clogged.

This is easily remedied by removing the drain tube and check valve, if so equipped. Clean the drain, the valve and be certain the hole in the block is clear of any obstructions. When all the obstructions have been removed, the cleaned components can be installed. Start the engine and check for a good air flow.

After this procedure is completed, the smoke may remain. With the engine under load the smoke should dissipate steadily, over the next hour. The exhaust should now be burning clean.

If your engine has ever stopped running, from lack of fuel, this next procedure will help get the engine up and running again.

Small amounts of air in the fuel supply lines can stop an engine from running. The smaller the engine the less tolerant it is of air in the system. Larger engines can, at times, pass small amounts of air through the system virtually unnoticed.

There are two circumstances which are the usual culprit, resulting in the lack of fuel to the engine. One is, no fuel in the tanks. Sounds simple, but is more common than one may first believe. This is easily remedied by adding more fuel to the tanks.

The other is a result of changing a fuel filter. When a filter is changed, the canister or spin-on filter should be filled with fuel, to prevent an air trap from forming inside the filter. This air can be drawn into the engine or locked in place in the filter. In either event the fuel can not by-pass the air. Therefore, the fuel flow to the engine is restricted or non-existent. The air must be removed in order to resume the full fuel flow to the engine.

The process of bleeding a fuel system, from the tank to

the filter, is explained in Chapter Three, *Fuel Supply Systems*. The following procedure is directed at the engine and the injectors.

There are several preliminary steps before the actual bleeding of the fuel system. Be certain the filters are full of fuel. The tanks must have sufficient fuel to cover the bottom of the pick up tube. You must gain access to the injectors, as described above for checking faulty injectors.

If the engine has a compression release valve, close the raw water seacock and open the compression release valve. If the engine has a priming pump, this can be used to force fuel into the injectors. If the engine does not have a priming pump, two people will be needed for the job, or a remote starter switch can be used. (Available at most auto supply houses.) One person must work at the engine and another will be needed to start and stop the starter motor.

CAUTION: Do not run the starter motor more than thirty seconds at a time. Allow the motor to cool for two minutes between uses.

Courtesy of Onan

Typical fuel transfer pump with manual priming lever.

Start with the forward most injector. Using the proper size wrench, loosen the fuel supply line to the injector. Use the priming pump or run the starter motor to turn the engine.

A mixture of air bubbles and fuel will begin to flow from the supply line. When this mixture becomes fuel only, with no visible air bubbles, tighten the fuel line fitting, while the fuel is still flowing. Do not stop the priming pump or the starter motor until the fitting is tight. Doing so may cause air to be vacuumed into the line.

When the first injector has air free fuel flowing to it, the next injector can be bled, using the same procedures. Continue to bleed the system until air free fuel is flowing from all of the injectors.

CAUTION: Use extreme care when using the starter motor to turn the engine. As more injectors have a good fuel supply, the likelihood of the engine firing increases. You can decrease this likelihood by restricting the air flow or opening the compression release valve.

Chapter Three, *Fuel Supply Systems,* will further discuss the fuel systems and fuel related concerns which cause engine problems.

Engine mechanics is not the top secret trade many would like boaters to believe. The work discussed in this chapter can be accomplished by most people that have the desire to learn how to save money on engine repair and maintenance. The one basic rule to follow is simple: It goes together the same way it came apart, with no extra parts.

CHAPTER TWO

GASOLINE ENGINES

Gasoline engines were the first engines considered to be a viable power plant for the recreational yacht. The steam engine, which preceded the gasoline engine, was a large bulky mass of very weighty metal. These features made it necessary to design the boats around the needs of the engine. The advent of affordable small engine power was a boom to the recreational boating business in the early part of this century.

Unlike its diesel counter part, the gasoline engine is limited in its functional horsepower output. This is derived from prohibitive operating and design costs. Not the inability of gasoline engines to produce high horsepower, as is proven by many racing boats.

Practicality, dependability and efficiency dictates the use of gasoline engines for horsepower requirements between two horsepower and four hundred horsepower. The engines are normally used in applications which require speed over engine longevity and lower per hour fuel costs.

Gasoline engines are not well suited to long periods of low rpm idle, such as trolling or battery charging at anchor. There cost per hour in fuel consumption is also increased over the diesel engine. These traits make a gasoline engine a poor choice for a cruising vessel.

One benefit of a gasoline engine is its low initial cost.

They are generally one half to one third the cost of a comparable diesel engine. This fact alone, makes them the choice of many weekend power boaters.

Courtesy of Volvo Penta

This new Volvo Penta TAMD22SX is typical of designs used for an I/O (Inboard/Outboard) gasoline power plant.

The inboard gasoline engine is an extremely complex piece of machinery. It is designed, built and manufactured within close tolerances which must be maintained. Keeping the engine within these tolerances will allow the engine to meet its design parameters of good performance and expected economy. Failure to maintain the engine according to the manufacturer's recommendations will start an irreversible degradation process which can only lead to the early demise of your engine.

The two most important maintenance procedures you can accomplish, for the long life of any engine are frequent oil changes and tune ups. Keeping this work on a proper schedule will dramatically increase the life of your engine.

An oil change and a tune up are generally completed at the same time. Before I discuss oil change procedures and tune ups, I would like to briefly mention a few considerations for your next refueling.

Fuel stabilizing additives will help lubricate and protect

the intake and exhaust valves. Be certain you purchase the type suitable for constant use, as some of these products are only meant for winter storage. Water absorption products will eliminate water from the fuel system. This, in turn, retards the wear on the intake and exhaust components which is inherent with water contaminated fuel. Chapter Three, Fuel Supply Systems, discusses this area in more detail.

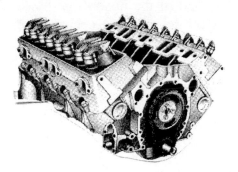

Internal components of a gasoline engine.

Oil is the life's blood of any engine. Without the proper amount, weight and type of oil, the engine is doomed. The owners manual for your engine will give you the recommended viscosity, type and oil change intervals in hours. Adhere to these recommendations above all else.

Regardless of the hours on the engine the oil must be changed at least every six months. Oil will break down over a six month period and loose a great deal of its lubricating ability. During winter storage a stabilizer may be added to maintain the oil's integrity. Decommissioning an engine, is discussed in detail in this book's companion, *Boat Repair Made Easy -- Haul Out.*

An oil change is not difficult to perform but it can be messy, if you are not diligent with details. There are a few items which will make the job considerable easier.

A filter wrench is necessary if you have spin on filters.

A hose running from the oil pan drain to a point well above the oil pan, should be installed if there is not one on the engine. This is accomplished, after the oil has been drained from the engine. The new hose will not help with this oil change, but future oil changes will be easier.

Remove the oil pan plug and install a barbed fitting, with matching thread size in the hole. The barbed end should accept a minimum of a 3/8" ID reinforced rubber hose. Double clamp the hose to the fitting.

The opposite end of the hose must be lead to a point above the top of the oil pan and secured with a retaining strap or clamp. A barbed fitting with female threads and a pipe plug must be double clamped in this end of the hose. When this hose is used to change the oil, the pipe plug is removed and an adapter threaded in place to accept the oil change pump hose.

This simple improvement will allow the oil to be pumped out of the engine and directly into a bucket for disposal. It eliminates the need to drain the oil into a container and then into the bucket for disposal.

There are many oil change pumps marketed with a 12 VDC pump mounted on a bucket. The inlet hose is run from the oil pan's pick up tube and the discharge hose drains into the bucket. They are expensive. Many manufacturers produce a hand pump with a tube which is inserted into the dipstick tube and the oil is pumped out of the pump into a bucket. This type of pump will rarely remove all the oil from the pan. The pick up tube of the pump, if inserted too far or not far enough, will generally miss the oil in the bottom of the pan. I prefer a simple electric drill pump, by Jabsco. This unit is attached to a drill with the hoses running the same as the 12 VDC pump. When the oil change is complete, the pump stores in a zip lock bag, taking little space.

If you believe your engine is contaminated with sludge from prior improper maintenance, the following process will help remove the sludge. Before warming the engine, add one quart of kerosene to the crankcase for every five quarts of engine oil, but never more than three quarts. Warm the engine to one half the normal running temperature, but not longer than ten minutes. Shut down the engine and change the oil as described below. Engines with an oil capacity of more than five quarts, should have an equal amount of oil drained before the kerosene is added. As an example, a ten quart system should have two quarts of oil drained, before adding the two quarts of kerosene.

The first step for any oil change is warming the engine to one half operating temperature. Shut down the engine and allow the oil to drain back into the pan, for a minimum of thirty minutes. Remove the oil filler cap. The oil can now be drained from the pan using one of the methods discussed above.

Remove the oil filter with a filter wrench, if it is a spin on design, and discard the filter. If the filter is a canister type, the element is inside a steel canister, loosen the canister and drain as much oil as possible, before removing the canister entirely.

A spin on filter is replaced by "spinning" it onto the mounting stud. Before the filter is installed, the rubber gasket must have a thin film of oil applied to it,. This step will allow the filter to be easily removed at the next oil change. Turn the filter onto the stud until the gasket makes contact with the base. After contacting the base the filter must be turned an additional one half to two thirds of a turn, (as stated on the filter) to provide the correct seal. Turning it further will make it difficult to remove and turning it less will allow it to leak.

After removing the canister type filter, remove the element from the canister and discard it properly. Clean the canister well, using a parts brush and diesel fuel or parts cleaner. Dry the inside and insert the new element. The rubber or fiber gasket, located where the rim of the canister contacted the base, must be replaced. This can be removed using a blunt tipped tool and prying it out of the base. Apply a film of oil to the new gasket and install the gasket.

Hold the canister in place with the stud protruding from

the top of the canister. Start the thread of the stud before positioning the canister itself. Caution must be used, to prevent cross-threading the stud. Turn the stud in until the canister has made contact with the gasket. Be certain to check the alignment of the canister to the base and snugly tighten the stud, but do not over tighten.

Some engine design engineers, I am certain, take great pleasure in locating the filter in an out of the way location and inverted. If this is the case with your engine, the best to hope for is catching most of the oil and cleaning the drip pan thoroughly, after the spill. There are remote oil filter location kits available which allows the oil filter to be moved to a more convenient location.

The next step is adding the correct amount of the proper viscosity and type of oil to the crankcase. Do not over fill the engine. I suggest using all but the last two quarts required. Then allow thirty minutes for the oil to drain into the pan. Check the oil level on the dipstick and add more oil if indicated.

The final step is checking for leaks. Start the engine and allow the oil pressure to build. Check the oil filter, oil pan drain and fill cap for signs of leaks. If there are leaks tighten the offending component, wipe the oil clean and check again. When all is leak free the engine can be shut down. Wait thirty minutes and check the engine oil level, it is not uncommon for the engine to require more oil after the initial run.

Considering adding a product such as Slick 50 during the oil change. This product significantly reduces wear at start-up and during long periods of slow idle, when oil pressure is low.

Changing a fuel filter is accomplished using the identical steps, outlined above, for the two types of oil filters, with these two exceptions. The gasket must be coated with a thin film of fuel oil, not motor oil. The filter must also be filled with fuel before its final installation. Failure to fill the filter with fuel may result in an air trap, which can only be removed by bleeding the engine's fuel system.

The first step for a complete tune up will be the purchase of a shop manual for your engine. Many after-market companies print these manuals to include most of the repairs you will need to accomplish on your engine. They also include valuable information such as capacities, torque settings, filter types and tune up specs to name a few. I do not know a single mechanic that does not own one of these books for each type of engine they repair.

A few steps should be taken to assure a professional quality job, both in performance and appearance. Start by warming the engine to one half operating temperature. When the engine has reached this temperature spray the carburetor cleaner into the carburetor. This will clean the fuel intake system of the carburetor, intake manifold and valves. The same product can be used on the exterior of the carburetor to clean off any residue or grime. Allow the engine to idle until the exhaust is burning clean at which time the engine should be shut down.

A clean engine has many advantages. It is easier to work on, easier to spot fluid leaks, it will run cooler and will appear professionally maintained. Still many people believe this simple step to be a waste of time. I do not agree in the least.

While the engine is still warm from cleaning the carburetor, use an engine cleaning product to remove all the grease, grime, and general crust from the outside of the engine. Be certain the carburetor and distributor are well covered before you apply this product to the engine. Follow the manufacturer's directions for the application and removal of the products you have chosen.

I do not suggest products which require the use of a hose to wash off the product and the dirt it has removed. If you do choose one of these, turn off all DC and unplug the AC power cord. Use *extreme caution* when spraying a hose in the engine room. You do not want water on wiring, electronic or electrical equipment.

After the engine has been cleaned and has had time to cool down, you can start the replacement of the different components. I have a routine I use for every engine I tune. I stay with this routine time and time again. In doing so I find I do not forget any of the necessary steps. I will relay my tune up routine which you can then adjust to your liking, but don't skip any of the steps I have included.

Start by setting the gap of the new plugs, using a feeler gauge or a gapping tool. The gapping tool loosely resembles a pair of pliers and is designed to keep the gap constant across the tip of the plug. Working on only one of the cylinders at a time, disconnect the plug wire, remove the old plug, install the new plug and reattach the plug wire. By working on one cylinder at a time you do not run the risk of connecting the plug wire to the wrong spark plug.

After all of the spark plugs have been changed, remove the distributor cap. Replace the points, condenser and rotor by disconnecting and installing only one component at a time. You may need an ignition wrench set and ignition screwdriver to complete this work. Be certain to use the small capsule of grease to lubricate the distributor cam lobes. (The part of the shaft on which the points ride.) If your engine has an electronic ignition you will not have the points and condenser to replace, only the rotor.

After the points are installed they will need to be adjusted. To accomplish this, the points must rest on the high side of the distributor shaft cam lobe. You can turn the engine, to get the points on the high side, by using the starting motor. Turning the engine key quickly to start and then quickly off will "bump" the engine. This will move the engine slightly, and may need repeated until the points rest on the high side. A large breaker bar and socket can be use on the front pulley nut to turn the crankshaft which will in turn move the engine. Be certain to turn the engine in the direction of its rotation. This can be determined by bumping the starter and noting the direction the engine turns. When this phase of the project is complete, check the nut to be certain it remains tight.

When the points are resting at the proper location, slightly loosen the screw holding the points in place. Slide the proper size feeler gauge between the two contact points on the point set and tighten the screw. Remove and reinsert the feeler gauge. As you are doing this you should not see any movement in the contact points, but you should feel a slight resistance as you move the feeler gauge blade between the contact points. Tighten the screw and check the gap.

The replacement distributor cap can now be installed without the wires attached. Hold the old cap, with the wires still attached, over the new cap. Be certain the screws and other components line up on both caps. Remove one wire at a time from the old cap and install it on the new cap, in the same location.

Setting the timing will require the use of a timing light. If you have not yet purchased a timing light be certain to buy one with a white strobe, you can not see the red strobe type in daylight. The harmonic balancing wheel will have a groove cut in it. This is a heavy cylinder of iron behind the pulley, on the front of the crankshaft. Mark this groove with white finger nail polish or chalk. The timing mark is located on the block of the engine near the top of the harmonic balancing wheel. The proper timing mark (degrees Before Top Dead Center, according to your shop manual) should also have finger nail polish or chalk applied.

Connect the timing light according to the directions supplied with the unit. Start the engine and allow it to smooth out at idle. Shine the blinking timing light at the timing mark. If the two lines of finger nail polish match, no further adjustment is needed. If they do not match, the timing will need to be adjusted.

Slightly loosen the bolt holding the distributor in place. This is usually a bolt through a clamp at the base of the distributor. Make a small turn of the distributor to be certain it will move, then turn it back to its original location. Shine the timing light at the timing mark. Slowly turn the distributor until the two marks you have made with the finger nail polish, match. Tighten the distributor and check the marks again. If they remain in line the timing is correct and the engine can be shut down.

There are two items which need to be replaced every few seasons, but are not considered part of a standard tune up.

The first of these are the spark plug wires. To replace these, simply remove and replace the wires, one at a time, until all the new wires are in place. Always use the small clamps and hold downs that keep the wires out of harm's way.

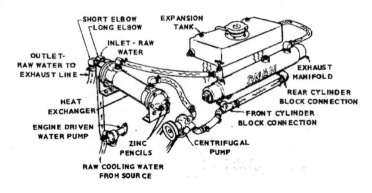

Courtesy of Onan

Fresh water cooling system which contains the coolant. System components will vary in size and shape as the engine's horsepower increases but the related system parts are basically the same.

The second, on a fresh water cooled engine, is the antifreeze/coolant. This, as with oil and fuel, breaks down after a certain amount of time and needs to be replaced to remain effective.

Remove the heat exchanger cap or expansion tank cap to view the antifreeze. Start the engine. Run the engine until you can see the fluid flowing in the heat exchanger or expansion tank. Add a flushing treatment, if needed, following the manufacturer's directions for its use. This treatment is only needed if the engine is running hot or there is poor circulation in the heat exchanger.

CAUTION: The coolant you are about to drain will be extremely hot!

Shut down the engine and drain the entire contents of the system, including the block. Most engines have drain cocks to facilitate draining the block. If they are frozen shut or nonexistent try disconnecting hoses to further drain the system. Close the drain cocks and connect the hoses. If a flushing treatment was used, fill the system with water only. Warm the engine, with the heat exchanger cap removed, and drain the system again.

Fill the system with the recommended mixture of antifreeze and water as stated on the antifreeze bottle or in your owner's manual. Start the engine and check for leaks while keeping a close eye on the coolant level. Top off the coolant and replace the cap.

When you have accomplished all the above procedures, you can consider the tune up of your engine complete and of a professional quality.

This work is not hard or complicated to complete yourself. It will only take a Saturday to complete the work on two engines, if you stay with the task at hand.

By doing this work yourself, you will not only feel more confident in your abilities to handle a breakdown at sea, but you will have saved more then one hundred dollars labor per engine.

CHAPTER THREE

FUEL SUPPLY SYSTEMS

Every engine requires the proper fuel in order to operate with in its design parameters. The higher the quality (not octane) of the fuel supplied to the engine, the higher the performance of the engine.

Do not be misled into thinking 104 octane flight fuel will increase the output of a small outboard. It will not. But a higher grade fuel, within reason, will decrease the chances of an untimely breakdown.

I refer to *quality* of the fuel as the condition of the fuel at the time of use. The *grade* of the fuel refers to its octane rating (gasoline rating) or cetane rating (diesel fuel rating) at the time of purchase. These are two extremely important points to remember as the subject of fuel is discussed. The grade rating of the fuel will be clearly labeled on the pump. The quality of the fuel is always suspect.

Normally, the gasoline rating for marine use will be Mid-Grade 89 octane, or higher. This Mid-Grade gasoline is a good compromise for the marina owner and their customers. It will service all but the highest powered boats on the water. Outside the U. S. you will be fortunate to find even 87 octane fuel and rarely will you find a higher octane rating. If your boat requires a high octane rating, it would be wise to have sufficient fuel on board for a round trip, before loading up the Scarab for a quick jaunt to Bimini for lunch.

The cetane rating may not be displayed, but in its place you will see Premium, Number 1 or Number 2 diesel fuel. Premium and Number 1 fuels are basically identical, but the Premium diesel may have additional additives included in the mixture. This is an important question to ask the attendant, as I will discuss shortly. Number 2 diesel fuel is a lower cetane rated fuel with more impurities than the other two grades of diesel fuel. Outside the U. S. it is the most common, if not the only grade of fuel you will find. This is not a significant problem. Most diesel engines are designed to run on any of the above mentioned grades of fuel. Most will, however, burn cleaner and more efficiently on one of the higher grades. If you must use a lesser grade of fuel, be certain to check your owner's manual for recommended oil change intervals when high sulfur fuel is used.

There are many safety concerns relating to the fuel system. These concerns must be taken into consideration during routine inspection and at each refueling. There are only slight differences, in these areas, between gasoline systems and diesel fuel systems.

It is wise to only use fuel system components designed for the type of fuel the boat consumes. These components are manufactured to withstand the reactions to the fuel for which they are designed. Diesel fuel components will work well in a diesel fuel system but may breakdown when used in a gasoline system. The reverse of this is also true.

When the boat is ready for refueling, a few safety precautions must be observed to lessen the risk of fire and the resulting explosion. These concerns are more prevalent to a gasoline powered boat but the diesel owner should also follow this advice to the letter.

Many marinas have a "What To Do When Refueling" poster hung near the pumping facilities. Read and follow this advice! I will list the common precautions the boater must take, each time the boat is refueled. This is not an all inclusive list, but as you will notice, these are commonsense answers to a potentially dangerous situation.

DO

DO - Extinguish all smoking materials.
DO - Extinguish all open flames.
DO - Shut down the engines and gensets.
DO - Close all windows and port lights.
DO - Have a fire extinguisher at the ready.
DO - Clean any spills immediately.
DO - Turn off all electronics, with the exception of a bilge vapor alarm.
DO - Turn off all electrical devices.
DO - Physically smell the enclosed areas of the cabin, engine room and bilge, before starting the engines.
DO - Vent the bilge thoroughly before starting the engines.

DO NOT

DO NOT - Use any cooking device.
DO NOT - Remove more than one fuel tank cap at a time.
DO NOT - Create a spark of any kind.
DO NOT - Turn on any electrical devices.
DO NOT - Turn off the bilge vapor alarm.
DO NOT - Hurry to fill the tanks. The next boat can wait for you to do the job safely.
DO NOT - Fail to make the above checks.

The following is a point of significant conflict. Many advocate running the bilge blowers while taking on fuel, suggesting this will constantly vent the vapor from any inadvertent mishap. Others suggest the blowers may cause a spark which will, in turn, ignite the vapors.

This much is true. Not running the blowers will increase the concentration of the vapors. Running the blowers will dissipate this concentration, but at the risk of a spark. This is an area where the boater must make their own decision, based on the layout of their boat and the method they are most comfortable using.

Two strongly suggested safety items are a vapor sensor alarm and an automatic fire suppression system.

A vapor sensor is not difficult to install. Follow the manufacturer's directions for the placement of the sensing and display units and the wiring for each component of the system. Another source of information on wiring DC are found in this book's companion, *Boat Repair Made Easy -- Systems*. This book discusses the proper wiring methods for any DC wring project.

Installing an automatic fire suppression system in the engine room and fuel tank area is an easy project to accomplish. The basic installation for all systems entails mounting a bracket and mounting the extinguisher unit in that bracket. The location must be away from high heat sources and clearly open to the entire area of protection.

There are options available for these automatic systems. One is the manual discharge option. Since the automatic activation is set to discharge the unit at approximately 180° you may find you would like to have the fire extinguished before that temperature is reached. Another option is a remote light. This light is wired to a normally closed switch, which means the red light always is on. If the system is activated, the red light goes out. I believe this is the opposite of the proper lighting, as most would more readily recognize a problem if the red light went on, not off. The plus side of the red light always being on, is knowing the system is operational.

I strongly suggest using Halon for this type system. If the system must activate, the Halon displaces the air thereby removing the oxygen needed for combustion. Unlike dry chemical systems, the Halon system does not leave a powder residue behind which can be a nightmare to clean. Another positive point for Halon is realized when you consider any of the chemicals used to suppress an engine room fire will be drawn into the air intake of a running engine. Dry chemical will cause significant problems within the engine, whereas Halon simply stops the engine from running, until the oxygen in the air is replaced.

These units are sized by the area they will protect. Therefore, it is important to accurately measure and calculate the cubic feet of air space in the engine room and the fuel tank areas. When the cubic footage of the area has been determined, use the sizing chart, supplied by the manufacturer or authorized dealer, to calculate the size unit you will need. If the engine room has power ventilation or diesel engines, it is wise to use one size larger than recommended. As I stated before, the system suppresses the fire by removing the oxygen from the air. If a diescl engine draws the Halon into the air intake or the power ventilators remove the Halon from the area quickly, the fire will not be suppressed.

A routine inspection of all the fuel system components is a mandatory ritual, which should be completed at a maximum interval of thirty days. This is the time to check the fuel tanks for signs of damage or fuel leakage. Check fuel delivery lines for signs of chafe, leakage, cracking, proper support and fitting integrity. Filters should be checked for signs of leakage, excess debris or water in the sediment bowl, fitting and seal integrity.

I will start with the fuel tanks and work towards the engine stating the areas to examine.

Tank seams and fittings are common weak points in the system and require close inspection. Gasoline tanks made of aluminum, have become an area of great concern in recent years. Failure of these tanks to contain the fuel as intended, has been the cause of many a disaster. The problem stems from the inadequate measures taken by many builders in providing thorough access to the tank for a complete inspection. Many times these tanks are installed in such a manner as to prevent any inspection whatsoever. In this case the owner can not inspect the tank's seams and connections to ascertain their integrity. When a seam or a fitting deteriorates to the point of failure, the gasoline will enter the bilge. This results in an extremely dangerous situation when the blowers are engaged or the engine started.

When inspection is impossible, sea water and electrolysis intrusion begin their inevitable damage. This damage remains unnoticed unless modifications are made to the boat which will enable the owner to thoroughly inspect the tanks.

The recommended remedy is replacement of the aluminum tanks with poly tanks, using a highly qualified professional. Be certain to insist on ample inspection access.

If replacing the tanks is not an option, you must be certain to thoroughly inspect the tanks regularly. This may require additional inspection access to the tank storage area, which may be as costly as replacing the tanks.

Always physically smell the bilge area for fuel vapors any time the boat is used, refueled or before the engines are started. Absolutely install a vapor sensor in the bilge and tank areas. The addition of an automatic fire extinguisher system, in the engine room and tank area, is strongly recommended.

The routine inspection of the fuel tanks should include a visible check of the seams and access plates. Check the seams for signs of leakage, corrosion and the plate's fasteners for tightness. The fuel supply line connections and vent line connections should also be checked for tightness and leaks.

The balance of the fuel lines should be checked from the tanks to the engine, including the filter system. As with the tank connections, be certain to inspect the fittings, and the exterior of the lines for chafe or cracking. This is particularly true at bulk heads or tight radius bends in the lines. It is not uncommon for a line running through a bulk head to wear through the exterior shield on the line. If this condition exists, replace the line and add a chafe guard to the new line. If any problems are evident, the correct repair must be made NOW! After the repair has been completed a thorough check of the repair should be made both at the dock and underway.

If, for no other reason and there are many, checking the fuel system regularly will provide piece of mind while you are on the water.

Bad fuel comes in many forms from simple dirt contaminates to large amounts of water. There are additives and filters designed to eliminate or reduce the effects these contaminates can have on your engine and fuel system.

As I mentioned earlier, the question of additives should always be asked of the fuel dock attendant. It is important to know what has been added to the fuel, by the marina or their fuel supplier, before you start adding your own ingredients.

As an example, adding a anti-algae agent such as BioBor®, to diesel fuel already containing such an agent, may break down the algae into extremely fine particles. These fine particles will pass through a ten micron fuel filter and clog the injectors. I encourage the use of additives in fuel to reduce the effects of unwanted material. However, as in most cases, too much of a good thing is never good.

Gasoline is the hardest fuel to store. It is meant for use within thirty days of its purchase. If you fill your tanks only two or three times a season, you should add a fuel stabilizer, such as, Star Brite EZ-To-Store EZ-To-Start Gasoline Stabilizer, to the gasoline each time you fuel the boat. As its name implies, it will stabilize the fuel which lessens the effects of degradation to the fuel.

Diesel fuel is not as prone to break down as is gasoline, but long term storage of the fuel will cause problems. Many diesel powered cruising boats have the capacity to store many hundreds of gallons on board. These boats may only consume one half to one gallon an hour while underway. They may also sit at anchor for weeks on end, using fuel only to charge the batteries. In this instance the fuel may last many months, degrading as the months go by. This is the perfect situation to use Star Brite EZ-To-Store EZ-To-Start Diesel Fuel Stabilizer, or similar product.

Water contamination is the most prominent problem of all fuels. The water may be introduced at the time of fueling or it may arise from condensation in the fuel tanks from temperature changes. Regardless of the form of introduction into the fuel system, the water must be removed before it reaches the engine. This can be accomplished by adding a water absorption product to the fuel tanks before the next refueling. There are numerous companies which produce such products and I have not found one to work better than another. All of these products combine with the water to form a combustible mixture which will pass through the engine and burn as fuel. My suggestion is to purchase the product which has the lowest cost per gallon treated, or use isopropyl alcohol. Isopropyl alcohol (a type of rubbing alcohol) is poured into the tank before adding the fuel at a rate of sixteen ounces for every one hundred and twenty-five gallons of fuel. Cost, fifty cents per pint, but isopropyl alcohol will not state "marine" on the label.

CAUTION: Add the water absorption products only as needed in gasoline fuel systems. Do not make this a standard refueling additive, particularly with smaller outboard engines. Be extremely cautious when using these products in small two or four cycle engines.

Algae's growth in diesel tanks is a common occurrence. The algae needs both water and fuel to sustain growth and this is commonly present in diesel fuel tanks. The algae can be killed using a product such as BioBor®. It will then be drawn into the fuel lines and must be filtered out with a ten micron or smaller filter. If the tanks are extremely contaminated with the growth, an ultrasound and exterior large filter cleaning system should be used by a qualified professional.

To lessen the algae growth, isopropyl alcohol, in the

ratio mentioned above, or another water absorption product, should be used to remove the water from the fuel tanks. Unlike gasoline engines, this can be added, in the correct proportions, with each refueling.

Cold climates and the resulting cold temperatures, present during early or late season boating, can cause diesel fuel to gel. When this occurs the fuel will not flow through the system. There are a few popular methods to prevent this gelling action in the fuel system. If you plan to keep the boat in service during cold weather, the easiest method is heating the boat. This not only stops the gelling of the fuel, but eliminates the need to take special precautions towards protection for the other systems which are temperature sensitive. It is not wise to place a heater of any type in the fuel storage area, but be certain the heat will be transmitted to that area.

Another method often used is a fuel additive. When mixed into the fuel and run through the system, these additives will stop the fuel from gelling. Read and follow the label directions carefully. These products vary in their ability to prevent gelling at various temperatures. One may prevent gelling to -30° F while others may only protect the fuel to 0° F. Personally, I would close the boat for winter, long before I need this protection.

The last method is a mixture of kerosene and diesel fuel. The common ratio of this mixture is fifty-fifty which will stop the gelling down to approximately -10° F. This formula has been used in the trucking industry for years, yet it is rarely used in the marine environment. One reason may be the ability to acquire kerosene on the water, which is not likely to happen. However, every town in a cold climate, has at least one heating oil company which delivers both diesel and kerosene. Calling one of these companies will almost assuredly gain you the fuel you need.

Although the additives can be used to turn water into a combustible mixture, stop fuel from gelling and kill the algae, filters remain a necessary part of the fuel system. Choosing the correct filters for your boat begins with the fuel type.

The best known and most easily obtainable filters are those by Racor. This company manufactures filter systems for both gasoline and diesel applications, from small outboards to unlimited horsepower diesel plants. These filters will remove water and with the proper element can remove particles to two microns. Every fuel filtering system should have a two micron filter as the last filter in-line before the engine's fuel pump. Other brands of filter systems are available, but I have not found a system which works with such reliability or is as widely accepted as the Racor brand.

The most common filter for a gasoline outboard or gasoline inboard, is a metal base with a spin on element. These are available to replace most original equipment elements and bases or a Racor system may be added to provide additional protection. Options such as primers, water sensor probes and heaters are available in the Racor system.

The turbine type system, which is the most commonly used filter for diesel fuel systems, has a canister with a drop in replacement cartage. This style provides for draining the water and sediment build up from the bottom of the filter's bowl.

Both gasoline and diesel systems must be sized according to the required fuel flow of the engine. Gasoline engines will require smaller filters since all of the fuel flowing into the engine is consumed. Diesel engines will require a higher capacity filter since the engine only consumes a small portion of the fuel supplied and the balance is returned to the tanks.

To properly size a diesel filter to the engine, request information from the engine manufacturer or consult your owner's manual for the amount of fuel supplied to the engine per hour.

Two useful formulas for sizing your fuel filters.

Gasoline engines. Maximum horsepower rating multiplied by 10% = Gallons Per Hour of fuel consumed. As an example, 200 HP x 10% = 20 GPH. This figure includes a safety margin.

Diesel fuel engines. Maximum horsepower rating multiplied by 0.36 = Gallons Per Hour which will pass through the filter. This is not the consumption rate of the engine as diesels will return up to 98% of the fuel to the fuel tank.

Courtesy of Racor

This turbine filter by Racor is the best unit for use in diesel applications.

If you have gasoline engines and would like to check the above for accuracy, the following method can be used. Fill the tanks and run at the usual speed for fifteen minutes. Fill the tanks again and multiply the gallons needed to refill the tanks by four. Add fifty percent to this figure. This will be the amount of fuel consumed in one hour plus a fifty percent safety margin. Base the filter capacity selection on this figure.

When the amount of fuel needed by the engine is determined, you must contact Racor or an authorized dealer. Request the information on sizing, types and options for their gasoline or diesel filters. Racor and most engine manufacturers are listed in *Appendix Two*, in this book. Filter selection information may also be acquired by contacting most of the major marine distributors.

The first step in the installation of a new filter system is reading, understanding and following all the directions and literature supplied with the unit of choice.

Be certain to use only brass fittings and hoses rated for the fuel they will carry. All of the fuel line and fuel line connection fittings must be flare fittings. Using this type fitting, will greatly reduce the chances of a fitting failure. I do not believe in the barbed fitting and hose clamp approach to fuel line installation.

When installing a new filter system, the fuel tanks may need to be drained to prevent a siphoning action of the fuel from the tanks. This may occur when the fuel supply line is disconnected from its current location. Be certain to close all of the fuel valves on the supply lines. If this is a diesel fuel system, close any fuel valves on the return lines.

DANGER: A certain amount of fuel will escape from the fittings as they are disconnected. It is prudent to extinguish all flames and turn off all power to the boat. This includes the batteries and the shore line. Have a fire extinguisher at the ready!

Mount the filter unit in a location which will provide good access for inspection and element replacement. Many times the fuel supply line, which is currently running to the engine or to the old filter, can be disconnected from that location. This line can then be connected to the inlet side of the new filter. If the length of the line is too short, an additional line may be added, using a flare union to connect the two lines. A new line can then be attached from the outlet side of the new filter to the engine connection point. All of the lines must be protected from moving machinery parts, chafe, water immersion, heat and wiring.

When a two or ten micron Racor filter is added to the system, it should be place in the fuel line to be the last filter the fuel will pass through before it reaches the engine. If the current filtering system is comprised of a thirty micron strainer and a ten micron filter a Racor with a two micron filter element should be used <u>after</u> the other two filters. If you want to continue to use the current filters, the fuel line can be run from the last filter, currently in the line, to the Racor and back the engine. Using this system will dramatically increase the filter life of the two micron Racor filter. Now it is used to filter only particles smaller than ten microns instead of filtering all the debris in the system.

To make a proper connection with a flare fitting, coat both fittings with a Teflon® pipe dope for lubrication. Avoid getting the pipe dope into the interior of the hose or the fittings. Pipe dope should also be used for all male and female threaded fittings. Hand tighten the fuel line flare fitting onto the filter flare fitting. (The fuel filter fitting may need an adapter to convert it to a flare fitting.) Using the proper size wrenches, hold the filter mounted fitting with one wrench and tighten the fuel line fitting with another wrench. Tighten the fitting until it is snug. Do not over tighten the fitting by exerting undo force. In other words, do not put everything you have behind the wrench.

When the new installation is complete, the filter and the new lines must be bled to remove trapped air. The filter to the engine portion of this process is covered in *Chapters One and Two*, as is the replacement of diesel and gasoline filter elements. Bleeding the system from the tanks to the filter will be discussed shortly.

Two common items replaced on a fuel supply system are the fuel gauge sending unit and a fuel line.

A fuel line is replaced, using the same steps and precautions as outlined above for installing a new filter system. The tanks may need to be drained to prevent a siphoning action when the line is disconnected.

With the safety precautions in place and all the valves closed, disconnect the line at the end closest to the tank. Be certain to catch as much of the fuel as is possible now and while draining the balance of the line. Disconnect the opposite end of the line. Prepare the fittings of the new line and its connection points and tighten the fittings as outlined above. This is an easy repair to complete yourself. The primary concerns are the safety aspects which must be adhered to at all times.

CAUTION: All of the same precautions and safety concerns addressed in the last two projects must again be used for this project.

Typical fuel sending unit for permanently mounted fuel tank.

To replace a fuel gauge sending unit in a tank, you must first gain access to the unit. If the entire top of the tank is visible, this is an easy chore. In most newer boats, this is not an easy operation. It may require cutting into a section of the decking or cabin sole to gain the needed access. If this is the case, a deck plate should be installed to allow future easy access. Caution must be used when cutting through the deck or cabin sole to eliminate the possibility of cutting into the top of the fuel tank.

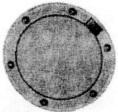

This style of deck plate can be installed to gain access to the fuel sending unit. Follow all manufacturer's instructions when installing the deck plate.

When the access has been gained, the fasteners and the wiring of the sending unit will be visible. Be certain all power is off to the 110 VAC and the 12 VDC systems. Disconnect the wiring, being certain to label which wire went where. Loosen the fasteners and remove the unit by pulling it straight up and out of the tank. This may require a little finesse, since the unit may be located between baffles in the tank. Slow and careful is the best method to use.

When the old unit is removed the new unit should have the adjustments made to it, using the old unit as a pattern. Most sending units are designed to fit a wide range of tank sizes. You must adjust the length of the float rod and possibly the angle of the rod in relationship to the top of the unit. Using the old unit as a guide, will make this process much more accurate.

When all the adjustments have been completed, coat both sides of the new gasket with petroleum jelly. Slide the gasket over the float end of the unit and place the unit into the tank, in exactly the same manner it was removed.

Snug the fasteners evenly until the gasket is compressed to show a very slight bulge at the fasteners. Connect the wiring, according to your labeling, and test the unit. Check the seal of the gasket the first time the boat is underway and again when the tanks are full. Any leaks will be readily noticeable and must be attended to NOW!

The first step in bleeding a fuel system is filling the fuel tank. If the cause of air in the system was due to running out of fuel, this may not be an option, but it will make the job easier, if possible. The weight of the fuel will help force it through the lines to the filters. The weight of the fuel also causes the siphoning effect, discussed earlier.

Many boats, if not most, have a priming pump located in the system. If this is the case, follow the manufacturer's directions for its use. In general, this will entail operating the pump while slightly loosening the fuel line fitting on the outlet side of the pump. This line will flow directly to the engine. Continue to use the priming pump to pump the fuel through the system, until all signs of air bubbles are eliminated. Tighten the fitting and this portion of the job for a gasoline engine is complete. If this is a diesel engine, follow the steps in *Chapter One* to bleed the balance of the engine.

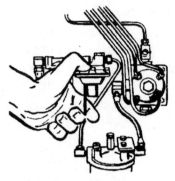

Courtesy of Onan

Manual priming lever on fuel transfer pump.

If your boat does not have a priming pump this procedure will help move the fuel through the lines. As I stated before, full fuel tanks will cause the pressure from the weight of the fuel to force fuel through the lines. Therefore, full tanks will be helpful for this procedure.

Slightly loosen the fuel line fitting on the inlet side of the first filter. This will allow the air to escape and the fuel, being pushed by its own weight, to take its place. When all signs of air bubbles, exiting the fuel line fitting, have been eliminated, tighten the fitting. If this is a diesel engine, follow the steps in *Chapter One* to bleed the balance of the engine. If this procedure does not work as intended, a more drastic approach is called for, which will require at least two people.

This procedure is accomplished by drawing fuel from a single tank. Be certain the fuel valve is in the position to draw the fuel from the tank you intend to use for this operation.

Remove the fuel tank vent line from the rear of the hull vent fitting. Install reducing fittings to facilitate the use of a schrader valve (this valve resembles a tire valve for an air hose chuck) at the end of the vent line. This may require several reducing bushings in order to step down to the schrader valve thread size.

With the valve installed, attach a bicycle pump to the valve. One person must now slightly loosen the fitting at the first filter while another person uses the pump to place air into the fuel tank. Pressurizing the tank will force the fuel through the fuel lines to the loosened fitting, where the trapped air will bleed out of the fitting. When all signs of air bubbles exiting the fuel line have been eliminated, the fitting can be tighten and the air released from the fuel tank. Reinstall the vent line as it was installed before it was disconnected. If this is a diesel engine, follow the steps in *Chapter One* to bleed the balance of the engine.

CAUTION: Never pressurize the tank to more than five psi. This amount of pressure is more than ample to force the fuel through the lines.

In an emergency situation, pressurizing the fuel tank with air, can be accomplished by a person with strong lungs and a true desire to get fuel into the lines. The vent line must be used for this type of pressurizing, as well. As each breath is blown into the vent line, place your tongue over the end of the vent line to prevent the air from escaping, while you draw your next breath. This must be repeated many times on even a small capacity tank. The less fuel in the tank and the larger the tank, the more air it will take to pressurize the tank to a suitable level.

CAUTION: This procedure can make you lightheaded. To lessen the effects of hyperventilation, breath normally every five to ten breaths. Most important of all, take your time.

When the fuel is flowing, air free, from the first filter in the fuel system, the steps outlined in *Chapters One and Two*, for bleeding the filters and the engine, can be accomplished. This step is needed only if air has been introduced into the fuel lines, between the filter and the engine.

The fuel system of your boat must be maintained to a great level of safety. When this level of safety is reached, you will also have a trouble free system. Water, algae and related debris in the fuel system can be extremely detrimental to the longevity of your engine. This, in turn, will also have a negative effect on the safety of the boat and its crew. Remember, a breakdown will only happen when there is no place to pull over and wait for a tow.

Good fuel, good maintenance, good filters and knowledge of the systems, as detailed herein, will increase safety while decreasing frustration. What more could one ask for from their boat?

CHAPTER FOUR

COOLING & EXHAUST SYSTEMS

At first glance, these two systems seem to have little in common. If we were discussing vehicles that would be true. Aboard most boats, however, these two systems are linked, each being reliant on the other to operate properly. If sea water for cooling is not provided, the exhaust system will not function as intended. If the exhaust system malfunctions, the cooling water will not be expelled overboard.

The above is true for all but the "dry exhaust" boats. The dry exhaust system is usually found only on work boats. The dirt and noise generated by this type of system is not conducive to the solitude most recreational boaters seek.

In general, these boats have an exhaust system similar to a truck or car. The exhaust is carried from the exhaust manifold through exhaust pipes and a muffler until it exits at a point well above the highest cabin level. The sea water used for cooling, is discharged overboard after it passes through the heat exchanger.

Marine cooling systems vary in design for the engines they are intended to cool. Within these variations there are two basic types; Seawater cooled or Raw Water Cooled (SWC or RWC) and Fresh Water Cooled (FWC). Sea water cooled engines have a greater tendency to fail prematurely than do fresh water cooled engines. The reasons for this will become clear as I discuss the two types in more detail.

A sea water cooled engine does not have a heat exchanger. The sea water is used directly by the engine for cooling. In this system sea water is carried from a through hull fitting, pumped throughout the engine's cooling ports and discharged from the engine. This discharge can take place via the exhaust or overboard discharge or a portion of both.

The sea water cooling system is a common system on I/O (Inboard/Outboard engines) powered day boats. These boats have an engine mounted inside the boat with an "outdrive", similar to an outboard engine's lower unit, mounted to the rear of the engine and extending through the transom. The water pick-up for the cooling system is in the lower portion of the outdrive unit. This is identical to the method used to circulate the cooling water of an outboard engine. Outboard engines are discussed in detail in Chapter Ten, *Outboards.*

The basic cooling and exhaust function of all outdrive units, for standard day boats are similar. A portion of the raw cooling water is used by the exhaust system to cool the expelled gases while the balance of the cooling water is discharged through the drive unit. The exhaust is also discharged through the drive unit which makes it difficult to discern the two forms of cooling water discharge. When the drive unit is in the down position, the turbulence at the drive unit, even at idle in neutral, will mask the two separate discharges completely.

Many of the higher performance boats with an I/O drive will have the exhaust exit at the transom above the water line. By doing so the back pressure on the exhaust is reduced thereby increasing the performance of the engine. The balance of the cooling water, the water not used to cool the exhaust, will exit through the drive unit.

Although raw water cooling of an engine is the most

economical means to provide cooling water for an engine, it has one major inherent flaw. <u>Salt Water Will Rust Steel!!</u> Boats used strictly in fresh water will have few problems with this type of cooling system, if proper maintenance is performed. Boats used in salt water, if only on occasion, will at some point, experience this problem but proper maintenance will increase the engine's longevity.

As I discussed, the sea water is picked up by the outdrive unit, circulated through the engine and discharged overboard. When the cooling water is salt water the inevitable happens. The interior of the block will begin to rust, and corrosive deposits will form. The scaling rust and corrosive deposits will block the cooling ports of the engine. The older the engine the more pronounced the blockage becomes. The engine will begin to run at a higher temperature, which is your cue to correct the problem. If the problem is not corrected, eventually the interior cooling ports will become completely blocked. When this occurs, the engine will dramatically overheat, seize and is most likely beyond repair.

To correct the problem before the engine is completely blocked, is a project for a qualified mechanic. This work will require knowledge of the entire engine and drive unit along with the proper materials and equipment needed to complete the repair. This may be a small project, such as replacing the risers and manifolds or flushing the engine. It is quite possible it will be as complex as "boiling the engine block" to remove the rust and corrosion. If the latter is the recommendation, be certain to ask the cost difference between this repair and the replacement cost for a rebuilt engine.

There is one simple yet rarely accomplished maintenance procedure which will increase the longevity of the engine. **Flush the engine after each use.** This procedure will reduce the residual material left in the engine after use. The residual material may include salt water, silt, microorganisms and in increasing areas, Zebra Mussels. This procedure should be accomplished regardless of the type of water in which your boat is used. It will work equally well for I/O, inboard or outboard engine units. The inboard engine requires a slightly different method which I will discuss shortly.

The first step to flush an I/O or an outboard engine is the purchase of "Earmuffs" (Outboard Motor Flushers). The muffs are place over the intake (pickup) on the drive unit. The intake is located directly below the cavitation plate on the lower unit. Attach a garden hose to the muffs. Turn the hose on to its full capacity. Start the engine and allow it to idle for ten minutes or until the temperature gauge indicates the engine is starting to run hot. Turn off the engine, then the hose.

This is easily accomplished with trailer boats which are removed from the water after each use. It is slightly more difficult if you slip your boat but it can still be accomplished. Raise the outdrive or outboard to its full up position and slip the muffs over the intake. Lower the unit and proceed with the above mentioned process. When the flush is complete, raise the unit again, disconnect the hose and muffs and leave the unit in the up position until the next use.

Flushing an inboard, raw water cooled engine will require an adapter to be placed in the intake water line between the sea cock and the sea water strainer. West Marine and other marine suppliers carry a device dedicated to this use. If this unit is too small for your engine's intake line, a similar device can be devised with standard plumbing parts. This can also be used on engines with a heat exchanger to flush the sea water from the raw water side of the cooling system.

With minor modifications, this device can also be used as an emergency bilge pump, should the need arise. A length of garden hose can be fitted with a strainer which is placed in the bilge. The opposite end of the garden hose is attached to the female garden hose fitting. If the need arises the valve is opened and the water is pumped from the bilge using the engine as the pump. The seacock may need to be closed, slightly to completely, depending on the engine's pumping capacity and the size of the hull breach. When using this device as an emergency bilge pump, be certain the engine has ample water flow to prevent over heating. Test the operation of this device at idle and slow running speed, before relying on it in an emergency. Knowing the best settings for the seacock valve will save time and stress if the device must be put into use during an emergency.

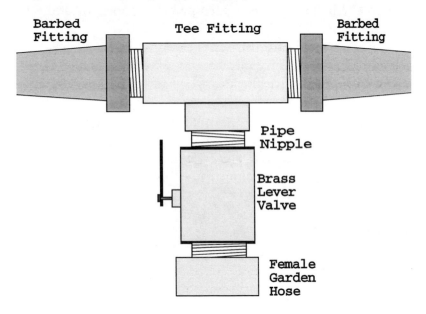

Refer to the illustration for a clear understanding of the design. Be certain to use Teflon® tape for all threaded connection, double clamp all hose connections and use only solid brass or stainless steel components.

To properly use this as a flushing device, connect a garden hose to the female garden hose fitting, close the sea cock, open the device's valve, turn on the hose and start the engine. When the flushing is complete, reverse the procedure and the engine is ready for service.

CAUTION: Be certain the water flow from the garden hose to the engine is sufficient to cool the engine. If the engine shows signs of overheating, the size of the garden hose may need to be increased. I recommend a one inch I. D. garden hose for engines over fifty horsepower. If your engine requires more than six gallons per minute of raw cooling water, this type of flushing may not work for your engine.

CAUTION: If your boat is in an area of the country where Zebra Mussels are present, it is suggested that hot water be use to flush the system. This may decrease the amount of idle time the engine can run until over heating occurs. A diligent eye on the temperature gauge is strongly recommended.

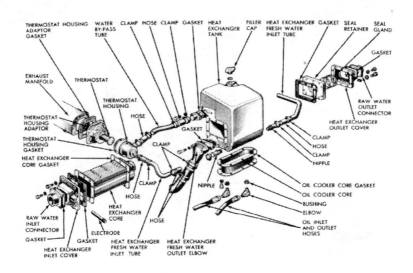

Courtesy of Detroit Diesel

Fresh water cooling system heat exchanger used in a diesel application.

The next type of cooling system to discuss is the Fresh Water Cooling system. This is the system most commonly found on inboard engines and gensets. If you are considering the purchase of any sizable vessel, this is a point to be considered, as I would not purchase any inboard powered boat which was not fresh water cooled.

The fresh water cooling system on any marine engine is

basically the same as the cooling system in a car. The radiator, in this case, is the heat exchanger. The heat dissipation method is sea water in place of the car's fan and forward motion air flow. Transmission and oil coolers have the heat removed by the same sea water as the heat exchanger uses. For all intents and purposes the sea water is your boat's air flow (fan).

Seawater intake through hull fitting and seacock with barbed fitting.

The sea water is brought into the system by means of a through hull fitting with a pick-up scoop (exterior strainer) mounted to the exterior of the hull. The through hull fitting has a sea cock to stop the flow of water, if needed. A flexible hose runs from the seacock to a sea water strainer and from the strainer to the raw water pump. At this point the engine manufacturer's design will vary as to the distribution of the sea water. In most engines it will flow to and through the heat exchanger. It may then travel to the transmission and oil coolers before being discharged overboard through the exhaust system and/or an overboard discharge. Some engines discharge all the water through the exhaust, while others use the enough raw water only to cool the exhaust and the balance is discharged overboard from a through hull fitting at or above the water line.

A variation to the above system includes the transmission and oil coolers on the fresh water side of the cooling system. This method uses the engine's coolant not sea water for heat dissipation. The transmission and oil cooling units are connected to the fresh water cooling system to facilitate the cooling. In this system the raw water enters the heat exchanger and is discharged upon its exit from the heat exchanger, using one of the methods above. It does not further flow through the system. If you have a choice of systems when upgrading the system or purchasing another boat, this is the system to use. The fewer components the sea water comes in contact with the less chance of the detrimental effect sea water will cause. If properly maintained, this type of system can provide twenty to thirty years of relatively trouble free service. This is far superior to the five to ten years with the other systems.

Vetus 1-1/2" plastic strainer for engine applications.

Proper maintenance for either of the above systems is not difficult. As discussed previously, flushing the system will help tremendously and can be accomplished using the above steps.

At each haul out be certain to clean the through hull fitting and its exterior strainer.

Cleaning the interior sea water strainer is a simple chore which will assure an adequate flow of raw water to the system. Many times sea grass, sand, silt and other debris will be present in the sea water strainer. The sea water strainer must be inspected and serviced on a regular basis to remove any restriction. If left unattended, this restriction can result in a simple inefficiency of the cooling system or a situation as severe as a damaging overheat shut down of an engine.

There are two basic designs for sea water strainers. One is designed with a bowl which is removable for access to the screen element. It is usually smaller and constructed of plastic. It is normally used for a head, air conditioning, wash down pump or refrigeration but may be found in use on small engines. Recently, several manufacturers have started production of a heavier built plastic strainer which is suitable for small engine applications. These strainers are similar to the Vetus strainer pictured on the previous page. Another design, commonly used for larger strainers, has a drain on the bottom, an interior removable screen element and a top plate. The top plate is screwed on or held in place with a large wing nut. This design is constructed from bronze components and is used mainly for high volume water flow demands, such as larger engines or gensets.

CAUTION: Before servicing any strainer, close the seacock!!

The disassembly of the small unit, is simply a matter of unscrewing the bowl and gently pulling the screen to loosen it from the base.

The bronze unit will require the removal of the drain plug, located on the base of the unit. When the water has drained from the strainer, the top can be removed by loosening and removing the wing-nut, on the top of the strainer or using a spanner wrench to remove the top. The screen may now be pulled straight up and out of the casing.

Clean the screen of the unit well. Use a soft tooth brush to remove stubborn debris. Clean the bowl with soapy water to remove any accumulated growth. If sediment remains in the bottom of the bronze strainer, use a garden hose, with good pressure, to flush the bowl thoroughly.

Assembly of either unit is accomplished by reversing the steps used to disassemble the unit. To provide a better seal and make future removal easier, use petroleum jelly or marine grease to lubricate the gaskets.

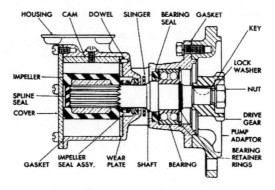

Courtesy of Detroit Diesel

Although raw water pumps vary in design this is typical of the most common types.

The next item in line is the raw water pump. This unit will wear with time and must be rebuilt with new bearings, seals, gaskets and impeller. All of these units are basically the same with subtle differences. I suggest purchasing a shop manual which describes the process for rebuilding the raw water pump for your engine. Read and understand the procedures as outlined in the manual and follow these guidelines. By doing so the project can be completed in two hours or less with professional results.

The impeller of many pumps can be replaced without removing the pump housing. If you choose this option, be certain to rebuild the entire pump, which includes the replacement of the seals and bearings, every second time the impeller is replaced.

The first step is the removal of the pump from the engine. This will be best illustrated in the shop manual, but the following will help you better understand the removal process.

Close the seacock. Remove both the inlet and the outlet hoses from the pump. Check these hoses for chafe, cracks or other signs of wear. If any deterioration is present, replace the hose with new wire reinforced water hose.

The pump will be held in place by two or more bolts. Remove these bolts using the proper size wrench or socket. Pull the pump straight away from the engine. If the pump will not move, the gasket may be holding it in place. Lightly tapping on the side of the pump body, using a brass or rubber hammer, should loosen the pump.

If the pump is separated from the engine but will not pull away from the engine, turn the pump body in each direction while pulling on the pump. Different engines use different drive adapters to connect the pump's shaft to the engine drive and this adapter may be holding the pump in place.

The pump can most easily be rebuilt if you have the use of a vise and a solid work surface. If a vise is not available, a friend can hold the pump body while the work is performed. A solid work surface can be anything from a work bench to a piece of wood laid on the deck. The work surface should not be metal as this may cause damage to the pump housing or its components.

When the pump has been removed from the engine, the cover plate of the pump can be removed. This will expose the impeller. If there is a snap ring clip in place to hold the impeller, the clip must be removed using a pair of snap ring pliers. Note the direction of the bend in the impeller fins. The impeller can be removed using needle nose pliers and pulling the impeller straight out of the pump body. If the needle nose pliers will not remove the impeller, use two screwdrivers, on opposite sides of the impeller, and pry up using equal pressure on each screwdriver.

The shaft will be held in place using a snap ring, pin or other retaining device. Regardless of the retaining method it must be removed before the shaft can be removed.

When the retaining device is removed the shaft can be pulled from the pump body. If the shaft does not readily pull out of the pump housing, a brass hammer can be used to drive the shaft out.

CAUTION: Be certain all retaining devices are removed before striking the shaft. Severe damage can result if this precaution is overlooked!

The seal and bearings may or may not come out with the shaft. If these components remained in the housing after the shaft is removed, they can be extracted using a brass bar and brass hammer to drive them out of the housing. Care must be used to avoid scoring or otherwise damaging the pump housing.

The cam resembles a bump in the housing where the impeller rides. It will only need replaced if it shows signs of wear or scoring. The cam will be held in place by one machine screw on the exterior of the housing. Removing this screw will allow you to lift the cam from the housing. It should be removed and cleaned if replacement is not necessary.

When all the components are removed from the housing, clean the housing to remove all debris and gasket remnants. The shaft should also be cleaned to remove any rust or other build up on the shaft. This can be accomplished using 400 grit wet sand paper. When all the parts are cleaned the pump is ready for assembly.

The assembly process is the exact opposite of the disassembly process. All the steps used to separate the pump's components can be reversed to assemble the pump. There are a few additional steps which will increase the longevity of the rebuild pump.

Before installing the new bearings be certain they are packed with grease. Many times the new bearings will be shipped "dry" and grease must be packed into the bearings. Use a water proof grease which can be found at most marine stores. Place a small amount of grease in the palm of your hand. Work the grease into the bearing by pushing the bearing's flat sides into the grease. When grease is forced into one side and an equal amount of grease exits the opposite side, the bearing has sufficient grease in-between the races.

The seal should have a light coating of grease applied to the mating surfaces to prevent corrosion. The spring side of the seal should face the same direction as before, usually facing the impeller.

The cam will only need replaced if it shows signs of wear. Coat the cam with a light coating of grease before installation.

The interior of the impeller housing and the impeller, must receive a coating of grease. This not only helps with the installation of the new impeller but also reduces initial wear. Use a pair of pliers, on the center of the impeller, to hold it firmly. Push the impeller into the housing while slowly turning it to bend the fins. This will aid in the installation by bending all the fins in the same direction. Be certain the fins are bent in the same direction as the old impeller.

The cover gasket should also be coated on both sides with a light coating of grease or petroleum jelly. Be certain all the holes in the gasket line up with the holes in the cover which must line up with the holes in the housing. The cover must be installed in the same orientation as before the removal of the cover.

Install the pump on the engine being certain every component is installed exactly as it was removed. Use a small amount of Permatex® on the gasket, engine and pump housing flange.

Connect all the hoses and open the seacock. Check your manual to ascertain if the pump will need primed. Many pumps will self prime while others must be primed before they will pump water.

Start the engine and carefully watch for the discharged

water from the exhaust, overboard discharge or both. The flow should be at least equal to or more abundant than prior to the rebuilding of the raw water pump. If water is not evident in one minute or less, shut down the engine. The reasons for the lack of water can be as simple as the pump loosing its prime or as difficult as a faulty rebuild. The appropriate repair steps must be taken to correct the problem before restarting the engine. Check for water leaks while the engine is running and after it has been shut down.

As with most things aboard a boat, the raw water pump will never breakdown at a convenient time. Rebuilding a water pump is a simple project that every boat owner should have the ability to accomplish. By having this ability you will know this work can be performed while away from the dock, providing you carry a spare pump kit on board.

Cooling water is now running from the inlet seacock through the cooling system of the boat and must be discharged overboard. This discharge will take place as a direct overboard discharge, discharged with the exhaust to help cool the exhaust or a combination of both methods may be used.

Most inboard engines will send at least a portion of the raw water to the risers where it will mix with the exhaust gases. The exhaust will be cooled by this mixing which allows the use of hoses and fiberglass fittings to carry the exhaust and water mixture through the boat, until it exits near the transom.

The following illustration shows three manifold and riser setups used by the respective manufacturers to mix the exhaust gases with the raw water and expel both overboard. Although these are all gasoline engine components, the basic design is also used for diesel engines.

A common problem with the Raw Water Cooled engine is the breakdown of the metal within the manifold and riser. When this occurs water will usually penetrate into the engine cylinders. The problem can be corrected without damage to the internal workings of the engine, if the problem is diagnosed and the correct repairs made immediately. This will entail the removal and replacement of the manifold and riser. This is not a complicated project to complete yourself but it can be time consuming.

Your shop manual will give you the information you will need to diagnose and complete this project and I will make the following suggestions.

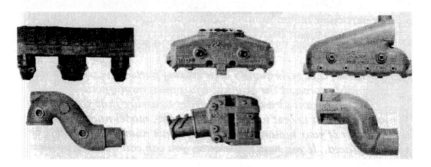

Manifold and riser assemblies from three manufacturers. From left to right: Chrysler, Mercruiser and Crusader.

There are certain symptoms which indicate the water is entering the cylinders of the engine. The most common is the lack of power caused by a non-firing cylinder. When water enters a cylinder, that cylinder cannot fire, therefore the engine loses power. It is wise to rule out the other common causes for power lose, faulty injector, poor fuel, water contaminated fuel, a general tune up, etc., before assuming the manifold or riser is the culprit. Other chapters in this book discuss these procedures in more detail.

The first symptom of a gasoline engine will be a slight oil sheen on the water at the exhaust exit. This sheen is caused by the unburned fuel from the non-firing cylinder. This is not, however, an indication for a diesel powered boat. Most diesel engines do expel a slight amount of fuel or oil with their exhaust, particularly when the engine is running cold.

When you are certain the other common causes are not at fault and you feel the manifold and riser is at fault, you can ascertain if the replacement is necessary, using this method. Remove the spark plugs or injectors from the engine. Using the starting motor, turn the engine until water is expelled through the spark plug or injector hole. If water is expelled from the cylinders, the manifold and riser should be removed, inspected and most likely replaced. Although there are other reasons water can enter the cylinders, a faulty manifold or riser is the most common reason.

CAUTION: Do not run the starter motor for more than thirty seconds at a time. Doing so can cause severe damage to the starting motor.

I always suggest replacing all the manifolds and risers on all the engines at the same time. There is a high probability if one manifold and riser is faulty the others are also or will soon become faulty.

When you are completing this project, be certain to accomplish the following. Use a high quality high temperature gasket sealant. Use all new bolts and washers. Spray paint the new components to match the engine. Change the engine oil and filter to remove any water contamination. Replace all the spark plugs or have the injectors tested for proper operation. These few steps will insure a high quality and reliable job.

As always read and understand the shop manual and instructions supplied with the new components. If you follow the above advice and the steps outlined in the mentioned literature you will have few problems with the diagnoses and replacement of the manifold and risers.

Water exiting the engine and mixing properly with the exhaust gases will travel through the last two components of the exhaust system. These are the muffler/silencer, if so equipped, and the exhaust hose or fiberglass tubing.

Marine exhaust hose must be used for the entire length of the run. Fiberglass components can and should be used to turn radius bends or to increase from one size hose to another.

CAUTION: Never decrease the size of an exhaust hose. This practice will increase the back pressure on the exhaust and a significant power lose could result.

The type of muffler or silencer to be used must be determined before the replacement of the hoses and fittings can begin.

The older style silencer is a horizontal cylinder with baffles in the interior of the cylinder. These baffles slightly restrict the exhaust flow and at the same time reduce the noise exiting the exhaust. They where an earlier attempt to quite the exhaust of larger engines. The new, quieter and much larger water lift mufflers of today have all but taken the place of silencers. The only exceptions are in older boats where the large water lift muffler can not be installed, in the limited space available.

Courtesy of Naqualift

Typical water lift muffler. These range in size from one inch ports to eight inch ports.

The water lift mufflers have an intake, a baffle in the interior and an exit port. The basic design is simple and extremely reliable. As water enters the unit it is held until it reaches the exit port baffle level and is then expelled from the unit. The exhaust noise exiting the boat is extremely quite. It is uncommon to here more than a whoosh as the water exits the exhaust. This is the main reason they have such popularity in the cruising community.

The main concern when installing a water lift muffler is the space needed to properly mount the unit and run the exhaust hose to and from the unit. Before purchasing any water lift muffler I strongly suggest contacting the manufacturer or your local marine supplier for the dimensions of the unit and the suggested free space needed around the unit. The literature supplied with the unit will give you the details for the mounting of the unit and connection of the exhaust hoses. When installing the unit, follow the instruction literature and the suggestions below for the installation of the hoses.

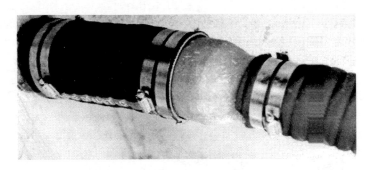

This fiberglass fitting is used to increase the size of the exhaust hose before it is attached to the transom pipe. Notice the positioning of the double clamps and the hose on the fitting.

To properly connect a marine exhaust hose to a fitting, the hose must first be cut to length. When measuring the hose, be certain to allow an ample amount to slide completely over the fitting and allow for any bends in the hose. The easiest and neatest method to use when cutting the hose will be the use of a hacksaw. The hacksaw will cut through the hose and the wire reinforcement within the plies of the hose. If the wire reinforcement causes difficulty, it may be cut with wire cutters or small bolt cutters. This is extremely expensive hose so caution must be used to measure and cut accurately.

When the hose has been cut it must be double clamped to the fitting. The fitting must be cleaned well to remove any residue from the previous piece of hose or from the manufacturing process. Next, slide the clamps over the hose, spray the fitting with a household cleaner, for lubrication, and slide the hose completely onto the fitting. The clamps should be tighten with the screws on opposite sides of the hose. This will provide equal pressure to the entire circumference of the connection. Carefully tighten the clamps using the proper size socket. Do not over-tighten the clamps as the undue strain may weaken the clamp.

Proper support of the fittings and hose can be accomplished in many ways. The hose should be supported at least every three feet and each fitting should have its own support. If you are refitting an existing installation, I suggest using the same methods which were in place when the system was removed, taking into consideration the above guidelines. If added support is needed, solid copper strapping or extra heavy nylon wire ties can be used and securely fastened with stainless steel pan head screws and, if needed, fender washers.

When all the components of the new exhaust system are in place and properly supported the engine can be started and the system checked for leaks. This is the final step in the installation or repair of the exhaust system. With all the above completed and checked you can be certain you will have few problems with the new installation.

Boat Repair Made Easy -- Haul Out, discusses other procedures specific to engine cooling and exhaust decommissioning and commissioning which must be accomplished when the boat is hauled out and stored. If any of these projects are in your boat's future, I suggest purchasing this companion book for a more thorough understanding of these procedures.

.

CHAPTER FIVE

MARINE REDUCTION GEAR

Marine Reduction Gears are referred to by several different terms. Marine gear, transmission, drive gear or marine reduction gear are the most common of these terms. If there is one correct term, it is *Marine Reduction Gear*, as this is the task the unit actually performs. However, the most common reference for the marine reduction gear is transmission. Therefore, I will use the term transmission as I discuss the unit.

The unit's function is to reduce the rpm's of the engine, change the direction of the prop's rotation and transform the engine's torque into a usable means of propulsion for the boat. Unlike a vehicle's transmission, with several forward gears, the marine transmission has only one forward. There is no need for more than one forward gear, as there are few hills on the water.

All transmissions reduce the engine rpm's at approximately a 2:1 gear ratio. This reduction ratio means for every two turns of the engine's crankshaft the prop shaft will turn one time. Most transmissions have the same gear ratio for the forward gear as for the reverse gear. The reduction transformation and direction changes, forward to reverse, are accomplished by a series of gears and plates within the unit.

The above is an extremely basic explanation into the workings of a marine reduction gear. I will not go into detail concerning the repair of these units, as this project must be left to a qualified professional. These units are as complex as any automotive automatic transmission and therefore, need the experience of a top professional. There are, however, several maintenance steps and simple repairs you can accomplish yourself. I strongly suggest purchasing a shop manual before beginning any work on your transmission. The shop manual will explain the time table and the steps needed to complete the routine maintenance and the simple repairs.

Courtesy of Detroit Diesel

Borg Warner Marine Reduction Gear.

The most important maintenance step a transmission requires, to run well, is checking the fluid level regularly. I suggest checking the level before each use of the boat. There will be a cap on the upper side of the unit. This cap will have a dipstick attached which has indicator marks for full and low. Some units require the engine to be running in order to achieve an accurate reading of the fluid level. Others require the engine be started, idled for five minutes and shut down to achieve an accurate reading. In either case, the reason for the procedure is to be certain the entire system is filled with fluid. This includes the hoses, filter and transmission cooler, if so equipped. Follow the suggestions in your shop manual to ascertain the correct procedures to obtain an accurate reading for your transmission.

CAUTION: Never overfill the transmission.

Each time the fluid level is checked, the transmission casing, hoses and cooler should be checked for signs of fluid leaks. This is an especially important check, if the transmission requires the fluid to be topped off regularly. If this is the case, one of the aforementioned components may be at fault, a seal may be leaking or the cooler may be leaking.

A leaking seal will leave a telltale spot or spray of transmission fluid at the offending seal. This leak must be attended to quickly, by a qualified professional. Allowing the leak to continue will endanger the transmission and may groove the shaft. This damage can be a costly undertaking. Therefore, it is wise to prevent the damage by making the repair quickly.

A leaking transmission cooler can be identified by a discoloration of the transmission fluid. The usual sign is a whitish tint on the dipstick which is an indication of a leaking transmission cooler. The sea water or fresh water coolant is entering the transmission by means of the cooling tubes, used in the transmission cooler. If this sign is found, the boat should not be used until the correct repairs have been made. This generally requires the replacement of the transmission cooling unit. This may or may not be a difficult repair, depending on the type of cooling system in use. The shop manual will be your best guide, when deciding if this is a project to accomplish yourself. When the cooler has been replaced, the transmission fluid must be changed, using the methods described below.

One item on the transmission which seems to receive constant abuse on many boats is the neutral switch. This switch prevents the engine from being started, if the transmission is not in neutral, thus preventing an inadvertent forward or reverse movement of the boat. The switch resembles a temperature or oil pressure sending unit and is often confused as one of the transmission sending units.

This switch is often mounted on the top rear portion of the transmission. In many boats, this is exactly the best place to step when going from the deck or cabin sole into the engine compartment. Stepping on the switch bends the contacts and may crimp the wires. When this occurs, the next step is straightening the contacts. This constant bending leads to fatigue of the metal and the contacts soon fail. When failure occurs the engine cannot be started.

Replacement of the switch is a simple matter. Remove the wires running to the unit. Inspect the connections on the wire ends and replace them with new connectors if they appear weak or deteriorated. Remove the old switch and install the new switch in its place. Reinstall the wiring and test start the engine.

The last maintenance item to discuss is changing the transmission fluid and cleaning the screen. This may not be a project you will be comfortable accomplishing yourself. It is not difficult, if you follow this general advice and the shop manual's procedures. All transmissions are different in their design. For this reason, I will only make general suggestions for this project. The shop manual will state the specific steps in the correct order for your transmission.

Start by draining the fluid from the unit, completely. When draining the unit, you should acquire at least ninety-five percent of the fluid the manual states it requires to fill the unit. As an example, if the unit requires five quarts of fluid to fill the unit to capacity, you should have drained at least four and three quarter quarts from the unit. If the unit is equipped with a filter this should now be removed. Remove the necessary components to gain access to the screen. Remove the screen and clean it thoroughly in a quality parts cleaning solution.

With the above accomplished the assembly process can begin. Start by installing the screen and the components which were removed to gain access to the screen. Be certain to apply a gasket sealer to any new gaskets before installing the gaskets. Install the filter, if so equipped, by placing a light film of transmission fluid on the filter's gasket. Turn the filter onto the stud until the gasket contacts the base. Turn the filter an additional one quarter to one third turn. For more information concerning the changing of filters see *Chapters One, Two and Three* in this book. Fill the transmission with eighty percent of the capacity needed. Check the dipstick. Add fluid, if needed, to bring the level to the full indicator on the dipstick. Start the engine to check for leaks and to distribute the fluid throughout the system. Check the level of the fluid, using the methods indicated in your shop manual. Add more fluid, if needed, and check again for leaks.

As I stated earlier in this chapter, there is little a boater should attempt to accomplish, regarding the repair of the transmission, other than routine maintenance. However, the one major project you may chose to attempt is the removal and replacement of the entire transmission. This project must be accomplished if the transmission requires extensive repair. By removing the transmission and delivering it to the repair shop, you will significantly reduce the labor charges on the final bill.

This project will require two people to lift the transmission from the engine room and load it into a vehicle. The weight of any transmission is at least one hundred and fifty pounds. The cramp spaces of the engine room and awkward working positions, will seemly increase the weight dramatically. Caution is always important when lifting or working with any heavy piece of equipment.

CAUTION: If your engine uses the transmission as a portion of its rear engine mounting system, DO NOT attempt this project yourself. The engine must be lifted, safely held in place, correctly lowered, mounted and aligned after the installation of the rebuilt transmission is complete. Fortunately, most engines do not use the transmission for its rear mounting.

Removal of the transmission will entail working most of

the day. The installation of the repaired transmission may require slightly more time. The first step is gaining the room around the transmission to work safely. Any component relating to another system, which may be in the work area or which could be damaged, should be removed to a safe location.

The propeller shaft must slide aft to allow the needed room for the removal of the transmission. Loosen and remove the shaft flange bolts. Push back on the shaft, while turning the shaft by hand or with a pipe wrench. As the shaft is turned it should move aft. You will want the shaft as far aft as is possible, to allow adequate work space.

The next step is draining the fluid from the transmission. When the fluid has been drained completely, the hoses can be removed. The ends of the hoses should be plugged with rags to prevent fluid leaks and debris intrusion. When all the hoses are safely out of the work area and above the level of the transmission, the wiring should be removed. This may entail one or more of the following items; the neutral switch, temperature sending unit or pressure sending unit. Next, the control cable should be loosened and removed from the area.

When all items have been disconnected from the transmission, the transmission can be loosened and removed. Start by blocking the transmission, from the bottom. This will prevent the transmission from falling off the engine and into the bilge. Loosen and remove all the mounting bolts. Be certain to check under the transmission for bolts not readily visible. When all the bolts are removed, pull the transmission straight away from the engine. This may be accomplished by hand or with the use of a pry bar placed between the engine and the transmission housing. Use the pry bar with caution, to avoid damage to the engine or transmission housing.

With the transmission resting securely on the blocking, carefully lift it out of the engine room. This can be most easily accomplished using a hoist. If a hoist is not available straps, lines or chain can be substituted with great care. **CAUTION** is the word when lifting this amount of weight.

Installing the repaired transmission is a simple matter of reversing the removal process. Lower the transmission onto the blocking in the engine room. Slide the transmission towards the engine, being certain to check the alignment of the engine and transmission shaft spline. The female spline of the engine and the male spline of the transmission must align exactly. Turning the rear flange of the transmission will have no effect on the front spline of the transmission. Therefore, this alignment must be checked and the adjustments made before the transmission can be mated with the engine. When the alignment is correct, gently slide the transmission into place and secure it with the bolts. Your shop manual will state any torque settings needed for the mounting bolts.

The wiring, hoses and control cables can be connected. The fluid can be added to the transmission.

Using the same method for moving the shaft aft, bring the shaft forward, until it mates with the aft flange of the transmission. Install and tighten the flange bolts.

Before starting the engine, check all the connections for leaks, the control cable for smooth operation and check the fluid level.

If the engine has not been moved the engine should not need aligned but the engine alignment should be checked before using the boat. This is covered in detail in this book's companion, *Boat Repair Made Easy -- Haul Out*.

Start the engine and use the correct methods for checking the fluid level. When the dipstick indicates the correct level has been reached, shut down the engine and check for signs of leakage.

The transmission can now be checked for smooth operation.

With the engine running and one person watching the shaft and transmission, put the transmission into its forward gear. Allow the forward gear to work for thirty seconds or more. Repeat this operation for the reverse gear. If all seems well a test run is the next step.

DO NOT run the engines more than three quarters throttle or the recommendation of the repair facility, for the first several hours of operation. It is wise to allow the new components time to break-in, before strenuous use.

A final word of caution. Any time a boat is underway the engine or engines must be running. If the boat must be towed or run with only one of the two engines, the prop shaft of the non-operating engine must be secured to prevent it from turning. If the shaft is allowed to turn with the engine shut down, the fluid is not being distributed throughout the transmission. This lack of fluid or fluid pressure can create severe damage to the internal workings of the transmission.

A small prop shaft can be secured by clamping Vise-Grips® on the shaft and allowing the handle of the Vise-Grips® to lie against the hull. Larger shafts can be secured using a length of line, wrapped several times around the shaft, and secured at each end to a solid object.

CAUTION: Always remove the securing device before starting the engine!!!!!!!

Above all else, when working on your transmission, be certain to read, understand and follow all the information in this chapter and your shop manual. The transmission of any boat is a complex yet reliable piece of machinery. A thorough and diligent maintenance routine will assure you of many years of trouble free service.

CHAPTER SIX

ENGINE ELECTRICAL SYSTEMS

The engine's electrical system is basic in its design and function. This system is intended to start the engine and monitor the engine's operating condition, while it is running. Other components, such as a stereo, VHF, etc., may come to life when the key is turned on, but this is merely a convenience for the owner. The electrical system of the engine is only concerned with the operation of the engine.

Although the alternator is an electrical device mounted on the engine, it is not involved in this system. The alternator's only function is battery charging. Alternators and battery charging are discussed in detail in this book's companion, *Boat Repair Made Easy -- Systems*.

The starting system of any boat is extremely simple to understand but not always easy to repair. The basic system brings power from the batteries to the starting motor. The starting motor's solenoid closes when the starting switch is activated. The power supplied to the solenoid activates the solenoid's piston. The gear on this piston is meshed into the flywheel gear. The starting motor turns the gear which turns the flywheel which turns the engine. When the engine starts the key is released and the solenoid piston gear retracts.

Most marine engine's starting circuits are wired in the same manner. Battery power is run from the starting batteries to a battery switch, from the battery switch to one or more solenoids. These solenoids often supply power to the engine monitors, accessories, etc. The battery wiring is then run to the starting motor's solenoid. When the key is in the on position, the first set of solenoids is activated and the power flow continues to the starting motor's solenoid. This becomes apparent when the gauges, lights, monitoring devices, or other accessories begin to operate. When the key is turned to the start position or the starter switch is pushed, a contact within the starter motor's solenoid closes. When this contact closes the power flow at the starter motor's solenoid is put to use to start the engine, as described above.

The starting system has four basic components which may require repair or replacement. They are the key switch or starter switch, solenoids, starting motor and the starting motor solenoid. Testing any of the components will require the use of a good digital volt meter, such as a Fluke. These meters are available at most hardware and electrical suppliers.

All of the test procedures below must be accomplished with the starting battery switch in the on position.

The solenoids are the easiest to check for operation. A helper must turn the key to the on position while you are near the solenoid in question. As the key is turned the solenoid will make a dead "thunk" sound, if it is working properly. If this sound is not heard, a further check must be made.

Check the battery's voltage at the battery using a volt meter, set to DC voltage. Note this reading. Next, place the red lead of the tester to the heavy side post of the solenoid which has the wire running to the starting motor. The black lead from the tester must connect to a good ground. Set the meter to read DC voltage. Turn the key to the on position and note the voltage. It must be within two percent of the battery voltage reading. If the reading is lower, check the opposite post of the solenoid. If the reading is low on this side as well, a faulty battery switch, wiring, isolator, etc. may be at fault. This is discussed in detail in this book's companion, *Boat Repair Made Easy -- Systems.*

If it is determined the solenoid must be replaced, use an exact replacement. Remove and label the wires as to their connection points. Remove the solenoid and take it with you to the supplier to match the new solenoid. Mount the new solenoid and connect the wires exactly as before.

To check the starting switch, set the meter to DC voltage. Place the black lead on a good ground. When the starting switch is off, the switch will have a hot and a dead lead. Check both leads, with the red lead from the meter, to determine which is hot with the switch off. Place the red lead from the meter to the dead side of the switch. Have a helper push the switch. The dead side should now show the same voltage reading as the hot side. If this is not the case, the switch must be replaced with an exact replacement.

A key switch will have more than two connection points on the switch. One will always be hot and the others will activate when the key is turned to the on and start positions. Use the above methods to determined which is hot. Turn the key to the on position and use the red test lead to find that connection point. Repeat the steps to find the start position connection point. If one of these connection points does not show a hot reading when the key is turned to the appropriate position, the key switch must be replaced.

Use the same methods as were used for the solenoid, to obtain the exact replacement and to connect the wires.

The last component which may have failed is the starting motor or its solenoid. If a "thunk" sound is not heard at the starter motor when the key is switched to start or the starter switch is activated, check the voltage at the positive battery cable stud on the rear of the solenoid or starting motor. If the voltage at the stud is correct, the starting motor must be removed and sent to a qualified repair facility for repair.

Removing the starting motor is always a difficult project. It will be located in one of the hardest areas to gain access and work.

Start by removing and labeling the wiring. Remove any bolts holding the starter in place, usually two or more bolts. Most starters are heavy, so caution is the key when removing the last bolt. Clean any grease and debris from the starting motor and deliver it to the repair facility.

Installing the rebuilt starting motor is no easier than the removal process, possibly, somewhat more difficult. Start by mounting the starter and securely tightening all the bolts. Install the wires as they were removed. Occasionally, space limitations require the wires be connected before the starter is installed. If this is the case for your starter, use extreme caution to avoid damage to the wires as the starter is installed.

When the starter is installed and all the wires connected, turn the key to test the unit. The engine should crank and start. If not, check the wiring, solenoids and switches again. It is rare, but occasionally a strong newly rebuilt starting motor will destroy another weak component.

Any time an electrical connection is removed it is wise to check the connection for corrosion or other signs of deterioration. Always replace any connection showing any signs of deterioration. This book's companion, *Boat Repair Made Easy -- Systems,* discusses the proper wiring for the batteries, battery switches, making proper connections and running the wiring in the correct manner.

Most engines have, at least, a rudimentary monitoring system to warn of low oil pressure and over-heating. The most elaborate monitoring systems will include these plus many others. There are systems, on the market, which will inform the boater of any system failure from low oil pressure to insufficient fuel flow.

Regardless of the extent of the system, the basic operation is the same. Sensors, dedicated to a particular monitoring activity, are wired into a control device. The monitoring system's panel, gauges, buzzers or warning lights are mounted in view of the helmsman. When a sensor detects a fault, the monitor shows the reading on the gauges or panel. A light may be displayed and a warning buzzer may sound.

A word of caution concerning these devices. Some systems are designed to automatically shut down the engine if certain sensors detect a certain fault. I do not suggest the use of this type of system without a delay present. This delay should allow the operator several seconds to make the shut down decision, based on the severity of the alarm and the boat's safety.

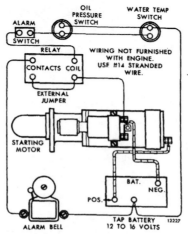

Courtesy of Detroit Diesel

This diagram shows a basic monitoring and alarm system. The starting motor is shown simply as a power source connection point to supply the system.

As an example: A boat is in the midst of entering an inlet with a strong opposing tide. The overheat sensor shuts down the engine without warning. The boat is adrift in a nasty situation with an engine which will not start. In this scenario, it is more than advantageous to have an overheating engine operating, than no engine at all. The damage to the engine may be severe, but the boat and her crew will live to complain about the engine repair bill.

The most common problems with any monitoring system are the connections and sensors. If a problem arises, which is not caused by one of the situations the system monitors, such as low oil pressure, then the monitoring system must be repaired.

The type of sensor can be determined from the monitoring system's manual or wiring schematic. If the manual is not available the following may help. Most alarm sensors are normally open (N.O.), they only close and sound an alarm when an adverse condition is present. Constant reading sensors (sending units) such as fuel flow, oil pressure and water temperature are normally closed (N.C.). Determining which type is which on the engine will remain difficult without a manual for the system. It may be helpful to trace the wires to their point of origin. If the wires from a sensor run to a helm gauge, which gives a constant reading, this is a normally closed sensor. If the wiring runs to the alarm system, it is usually a normally open sensor.

The first step is checking all the wiring connections to be certain none are deteriorated in any way. If deterioration is found the connection should be repaired and the system tested before testing any sensors. If the wiring is not at fault, test the voltage at each sensor. One side of the sensor should read the proper voltage while the other side will be dead. This is true for normally open (N.O.) sensor switches. Normally closed (N.C.) sensor switches should have a voltage reading on both connections. If any sensor does not show the correct reading, it should be considered for replacement.

Replacing a sensor is much easier than finding the sensor at fault. When your testing is complete and the offending sensors identified, remove the wires from the unit. Most sensors are removed by turning the sensor as you would a bolt. When the sensor has been removed, use a pipe plug or other object to plug the hole in the engine. Many times, when the sensor is removed, the fluid the sensor is responsible for monitoring will flow from the engine.

CAUTION: Exact replacement sensors must be used. These units have certain limits which match your engine's requirements. Failure to install an exact replacement may cause severe engine damage.

Install the new sensor by applying a small amount of Teflon® paste or tape to the threads of the unit. Turn the sensor into the opening, snugly. Do not over tighten the unit! Connect the wiring and test the system. If the system is not operating properly, further testing and replacement may be necessary.

Depending on the complexity of the monitoring system and its related components this repair can be easy and quick or extremely frustrating. Locating the offending components is always the most time consuming phase of the repair.

As I stated in the beginning of this chapter the engine's electrical system is a simple system to understand. As you have found throughout this chapter, it can be a frustrating system to diagnose and repair. A great deal of patience and a little luck will assure a safe and reliable system. Be kind to yourself and don't push hard to get these repairs completed. In this instance, patience is a virtue.

CHAPTER SEVEN

ENGINE DRIVEN ACCESSORIES

Every boat, regardless of its intended use, will have an engine driven accessory mounted on the engine. This accessory can be as simple as an alternator, which will charge the engine battery, to a full array of various system's units. A few of the more common engine driven accessories, aboard cruising boats, are large alternators, refrigeration compressors, water maker pumps, and A/C generators. These systems are discussed in detail in this book's companion, *Boat Repair Made Easy -- Systems*.

When these components are mounted on the engine, the convenience for the boater is increased. Running the engine for an hour, once or twice, daily will charge the batteries, cool the refrigerator, make water and provide A/C power.

There are certain concerns that must be realized before adding any accessory which the engine must drive. The first of these concerns, is the amount of horsepower the unit will require to operate. Many boats have the engine sized to push it, unlaidened, through the water, at hull speed. This design logic saves the builder money but at a cost to the owner. As the boat is laidened with equipment and belongings, it may not have sufficient power to push through a hard running current. Add engine driven accessories into this formula and, most assuredly, the engine will be burdened to the point exhaustion.

To better illustrate the above, I will relay a short story. A fellow boater ask my opinion to confirm or discount his mechanic's thoughts on adding accessories to his engine. He was outfitting to cruise and therefore, needed reliable systems. The forty-two foot sloop with an eighteen horse diesel engine, was large enough to cruise but it was designed, built and powered to be a weekend sailor.

After his belongings were aboard, the water line had to be raised five inches. This amount of weight and additional wetted surface, increased the horsepower required to propel the boat. His list of engine driven accessories included the standard cruiser's package of a large alternator, refrigeration compressor and water maker pump. Still more horsepower would be required to drive these components.

I made a few rough calculations. The boat would require an engine of at least double the horsepower to propel the boat, drive the accessories and have a safety margin for hard currents. In his mind, this was not the correct answer. After asking several repair facilities, the answers his mechanic and I gave him become a little more clear. In short, he would be lucky to get out of the slip.

The decision was made to lighten the load of the boat, use DC powered accessories and a large alternator on the engine to charge larger battery banks. This provided him with all the comforts he desired and a small margin of extra power.

The above example clearly shows the need to calculate the requirements of each accessory, before the installation.

When the calculations are complete and you are certain the engine can handle the extra load, one concern remains. Does the engine have sufficient space and pulley capacity to mount and drive the units.

The units will vary in physical size between the different manufacturers. It is wise to contact the companies you are considering and request their literature regarding the mounting, sizing and drive types available.

Most units will require a separate or combined belt to drive the unit. The above literature will state the available options. In general, large alternators, water maker pumps and A/C generators will require two belts to drive the unit. The refrigeration compressor may only require one belt. It is necessary to check the engine to ascertain if additional pulleys may be required. Adding or changing pulleys can be costly.

If all is within acceptable limits, to this point, the units can be purchased and installed. The manufacturer will provide detail installation instructions, with the equipment. They will also provide a package of adapters to facilitate mounting the unit on your engine. This package may include parts for other engines and different mounting methods. This is one rare occasion when left over parts becomes normal. Even with all this equipment, you may find the need to purchase a few items at the local hardware store. The manufacturer cannot take into account, all the situations which could be encountered on every engine. Above all else, be certain to read and understand all the literature provided with the unit.

Mounting the unit on the engine will take time and patience. Do not hurry this process! A few precautions should be taken when mounting the units.

Mount the unit securely. When all the mounting components have been installed the unit should have little movement.

Each separate unit should have an independent means with which to tighten the drive belt for that unit. With this type of installation, if a unit must be removed for repair, the engine and remaining units can be still be operated. This may require the use of a different belt to drive the remaining units but they will remain functional.

Be certain the drive pulley on the engine and the pulley on the unit, are in-line with each other. The slightest angle will rapidly deteriorate the belts.

Do not over-tighten the belts. This places undue strain on the shaft bearings of the unit and will lead to premature failure of the bearings. The belts should be tightened to a point that prevents the belts from slipping on the pulley. New belts will stretch after the initial use. Run the engine for several hours, check and if necessary, tighten the belts.

Before starting the engine, to test the new installation, be certain to check every component of the system, once more. I am constantly surprised, at seemingly obvious errors, which are not noticed until the engine is started and the damage has occurred. Completing one final check will reduce the likelihood of this occurrence.

After a new installation, I suggest letting the engine compartment open the first few times the engine is operated. This will allow you to hear any unusual sounds and readily view the new unit, to be certain all is operating as intended.

The engine driven accessories are truly a convenience to the cruising boater. However, if the above precautions are not considered, you may have a well-outfitted cruising boat which does not have the power to leave the slip. Make comparisons between engine driven and DC powered equipment. Taking the time to consider all the options available to you, will most assuredly provide piece of mind.

I suggest reading this book's companion *Boat Repair Made Easy -- Systems*. This will provide a more thorough understanding of these systems. The more information you have available, the less opportunity for a poor decision. Follow the installation literature supplied with the unit and the information contained herein. By doing so, you will be assured of a professional installation of the new systems.

CHAPTER EIGHT

THE ENGINE ROOM

Engine rooms range in size from the luxurious walk-in engine rooms found on large motoryachts to the small engine compartment of a day sailor. Though the size difference may be tremendous, the function remains the same, to house the working machinery of the boat.

Aboard most boats, the engine room is the location for many other systems as well. This is one of the concerns a gasoline powered boat owner must realize. Any electrical device located in the engine room must be ignition protected. This is to say, it can not produce a spark capable of igniting gasoline vapors. A device as simple as the contacts within a fresh water pressure pump can create just such a spark. Extreme caution must be used when installing any piece of equipment in the engine room of a gasoline powered boat. Diesel powered boats are not as susceptible to these problems. However, it is wise to use caution when choosing the location of any equipment aboard any boat.

Before I discuss the components which should be installed in a well-found engine room, I will discuss the equipment which should not be located in the engine room. The temperature extremes in an engine room provide a harsh environment for air conditioning units, batteries, battery chargers, inverters and other temperature sensitive equipment.

The air conditioning units must overcome the ambient temperature before they can start cooling the air. The compressor will run hot and the raw water cooling will not be as effective.

Batteries are affected by the heat as well. The battery voltage may read 12.75 VDC at one hundred degrees and at seventy degrees, but the state of charge (the amount of amp hours remaining in the battery) is significantly different. Battery chargers read the voltage of the battery to determine its state of charge. The temperature extremes of an engine room will affect the voltage reading and consequently the charging rate. This will inevitably cause an early demise to the most rugged of battery banks. Add to this the fact that chargers and inverters operate at a reduced efficiency level in a hot engine room, and it becomes apparent, the batteries will suffer.

The above are the most common items found in engine rooms which could be better placed elsewhere. *Boat Repair Made Easy -- Systems*, discusses the working aspects of these systems in detail. *Boat Repair Made Easy -- Systems*, will help with the proper placement and installation of any new equipment.

A well cared for engine room will be clean and neat. The tools and supplies will be stowed properly and secured well. The first step in this process is cleaning the engines to remove all the grease, grime and debris. *Chapter One and Chapter Two* of this book describe the cleaning process for an engine. The engine room can be cleaned using degreasing products, a shop vac and household cleaners.

CAUTION: Do not allow liquids to come in contact with electrical wiring, devices or equipment.

When the engine room is clean your attention can be turned to the bilge. You may wish to try one of the many products on the market for cleaning the bilge. I have not found one product to be superior to another. If you prefer a home remedy, the following formula will make a strong cleaner.

CAUTION: Wear a respirator, safety goggles and heavy rubber gloves while working with this solution. Mix this solution in a five gallon <u>plastic</u> bucket.

Start by adding one gallon of hot water. Stir in five pounds of TSP (tri-sodium phosphate) being certain it is completely dissolved in the water. Add one large bottle of concentrated lemon juice, as an odor eliminator. Add two gallons of chlorine bleach. Add hot water to bring the contents to four gallons.

Open all the windows, hatches and ports in the boat. Open all the bilge access points. Pour the solution into any bilge area that can be accessed. Allow the solution to work for a day or more. The rocking of the boat will agitate the solution and clean the bilge. Do not pump this solution overboard. Collect the solution by removing a bilge pump line from the through hull fitting and allowing the bilge pump to pump the solution into a bucket. The solution should then be taken to a proper disposal point. If the bilge is extremely grimy a second application may be necessary.

CAUTION: Do not allow water to come in contact with electrical wiring, devices or equipment.

After the bilge is clean, place an oil absorbing bilge pillow in the lowest part of the bilge. Use caution to avoid interfering with any bilge pump. Oil absorbing mats should also be placed under the engine to retain any oil which may leak from the engine.

Wiring, water lines and waste hoses should be securely fastened in place. They should be kept away and protected from heat, water and vibration. The proper methods, for this support and securing, are discussed in detail in this book's companion, *Boat Repair Made Easy -- Systems*.

Engine room ventilation is an important part of safety and the performance of your engine. USCG requirements state that any boat built after July 31, 1980, that uses gasoline for fuel and has an enclosed engine compartment, must have mechanical means to ventilate the engine room area. In common terms, this simply states the engine room must have a bilge blower.

There are two basic designs for bilge blowers. The squirrel cage style and the in-line style. The main concern is which will work in your mounting situation as both types are made in multiple capacities.

To properly size the blower or blowers needed for your engine room, measure the cubic footage of the area. Use this formula to arrive at the cubic feet of space: Length x Width x Height = Total cubic feet of engine room space x one hundred and fifty percent = the C.F.M. (cubic feet per minute) of the blower. Take all measurements to the next greatest foot. As an example: an engine room 9' 6" in length by 6' 8" in width by 3' high would equate to 10 x 7 x 3 = 210 x 1.50 = 315 C.F.M. The capacity of the blower must be equal to or greater than this number. Larger engine rooms will require more than one blower unit.

After sizing the unit, the unit can be mounted following the manufacturer's recommendation. The proper wiring techniques can be found in this book's companion *Boat Repair Made Easy -- Systems*.

With the blower installed, the air can be removed from the engine room, only if there is incoming air. The blower will only exhaust air if the air is being replaced with fresh air. This requires an incoming air vent of the same or larger size. If the boat has two four inch blowers exhausting the air, it must have two four inch openings to allow air into the engine room.

If you feel your engine room needs greater ventilation than is currently available, do not be tempted to use the incoming air vent for another blower unit. Additional exhaust and incoming air vents must be installed.

All engines require air for combustion. The more free flow of air that is available to the engine, the higher the combustion rate. This is particularly true for diesel engines.

Diesel engines require a tremendous amount of air to run at peak efficiency. The larger the engine the more air it requires. It is not uncommon to see a large vent, for incoming air flow, in the hull of a diesel powered boat. Unlike a gasoline powered boat, blowers are rare in diesel applications. Static ventilation is used for the engine room and to provide air for the engines. Static, meaning an open vent with no mechanical means of air circulation. The engine itself will draw the air into the engine.

The blowers are not needed to exhaust the air, as diesel vapors have a significantly higher flash point than do gasoline vapors. However it is a wise choice to install a blower and a vapor sensor in the engine room and fuel storage areas. This is discussed in more detail in Chapter Three, *Fuel Supply Systems,* in this book.

The engine room should be clean, properly vented, protected from fumes and all stray wires and hoses in their place. If this has been accomplished you will be proud to show anyone the engine room of your boat.

CHAPTER NINE

GENSETS

The term *Genset* refers to an electrical generator used in any type of application. Marine genset (generators), used aboard boats, provide power for the A/C electrical needs of the boat. Other common uses for non-marine generators are construction sites, back-up power for buildings and main power for homes located outside power plant distribution grids. While all these generators are basically the same, with the exception of their output, the marine generator has several unique features which set it apart from land based generators.

The major difference of marine generators is the cooling and exhaust systems used on the unit. These systems will normally contain the same components as a marine engine. These systems are discussed in detail in *Chapter Four* of this book. More subtle differences will be found in the wiring, controls and connectors, used within the unit. All of these components are built to marine standards which will provide a longer life span, in the marine environment.

This chapter will not discuss the engine portion of the genset. *Chapters One and Two,* discuss the engines in detail. Therefore, there is little need to repeat the information in this chapter.

This book's companion, *Boat Repair Made Easy -- Systems*, states alternative methods of producing power.

These methods may reduce the needed output of the generator or possibly eliminate the need for a generator. The book also has several charts and formulas which should be referred to when sizing a generator or alternative power sources.

The first step in generator selection, for replacement or a new installation, is sizing the unit to the current and future needs. I suggest consulting with a qualified professional before purchasing any unit. They can help calculate the correct output, physical sizing, cooling and exhaust requirements, for the units they carry. It is wise to contact several manufacturers, to determine which builds the unit best suited to your needs.

The following questions must be answered before a final decision can be reached.

The size and weight of the unit are critical for the placement of the unit in the boat.

The output of the unit must be known in order to size the unit to the power requirements of the boat.

Availability of parts becomes an important issue, if your boat relies on the generator for systems support.

Living aboard and cruising requires different consideration than a weekend boat. The question in this situation is: How many hours a day will the generator run and will the unit withstand this type of usage.

The unit must be fueled by the same fuel the main engines requires. It is a poor choice to use a gasoline generator in a diesel powered boat. The opposite is also true.

The noise characteristics, of a generator, are one of the important creature comfort questions. The decibel level without a sound shield and with a sound shield should be investigated. It is not uncommon for space limitations to rule out the use of a sound shield around the generator.

The unit must have easy service access to check the oil and coolant levels, change the water pump impeller, change the fuel filter, oil and oil filter. This access must be equally easy with and without the sound shield in place. If the sound shield must be completely removed to accomplish any of the above, the projects will, most likely, not be completed on a regular basis.

The above is not an all encompassing list of the questions which must be answered, but it does indicate the most often encountered installation concerns.

The physical size of the unit is dependent on the output wattage of the unit. The higher the output of the unit, the larger the physical size of the unit. Both of these concerns must be taken into consideration when choosing a generator.

In general, if a boat has one thirty amp shore line, the generator should be a four thousand watt unit. A fifty amp shore line will require a six thousand watt unit. Twin thirty amp shore lines will require a seven to eight thousand watt unit. As the wattage increases, so does the size of the unit. An eight thousand watt unit may be as large as the main engine. Add to this a sound shield and the space required becomes a vital concern for placement of the unit.

The weight of the unit will have a direct bearing on the placement of the unit. If the unit cannot be placed on the centerline of the boat, the weight factor is more critical. Placing a thousand pound generator to one side of the center-line of the boat will cause a significant list. This amount of list cannot be offset with opposing ballast. Placing the unit too far forward will create a bow heavy boat. Placing it too far aft will force the boat to squat in the water, when it is underway. In this situation the boat may not be capable of achieving a planing attitude while underway.

All the above facts equate to one simple solution. Consult a qualified professional before the purchase and installation of any generator.

When the proper unit has been selected the installation of the unit can begin. If this is not an exact replacement of an existing unit the only choice is having a professional install the unit. This is not a do-it-yourself project. The equipment, materials, tools and knowledge required to properly install any generator, is normally, beyond the capabilities of the boat owner. If this is an exact replacement of an existing unit and you choose to accomplish the project yourself, the following should be considered.

The project will require at least two people. You will need a means to lift the old generator out of its location and to lower the new generator into place. You will also need the correct tools and supplies to install the new mountings, wiring, cooling, exhaust, muffler and controls. Follow the manufacturer's instructional literature for the installation of the above. If the unit's literature does not include a shop manual, purchase, read and understand the shop manual, before you begin the installation.

The correct wiring methods are discussed in this book's companion, *Boat Repair Made Easy -- Systems*. The cooling system, exhaust system, fuel system and engine are discussed in the first four chapters of this book.

Generators are the most abused mechanical device installed on board most boats. If the generator is properly maintained and slightly pampered it will run well, but the occasional breakdown is always to be expected. Repairing these breakdowns can be accomplished by most boat owners.

The purchase of a shop manual for your unit, and a high quality digital multi-meter is the first step in the repair process. It is beyond the scope of this, or any book, to list all the repair steps of even the most popular brands of genera-tors. Each manufacturer uses different controls and circuitry to maintain the peak performance of their units.

One area many manufacturers now have in common is the use of circuit boards for most of the control functions. If a certain aspect of the unit is malfunctioning, a circuit board change may be the required repair. While this saves time and labor cost, the boards are far more expensive than the old style contacts or solenoids. Such is progress.

I have not discussed portable generators in the above as they are not a wise choice for most boats. The smaller suitcase units are fine as a back-up for minimum interim power, while the main generator is being repaired. This is the only duty for a portable generator aboard a boat. Using a large unit to supply the boat's A/C needs is not an advisable application. These units are not built for the marine environment. They are extremely noisy, costly to operate and not intended for constant operation.

The final choice for the type, size and installation of a generator should only be made after the proper questions have been answered. Pushing yourself to a quick decision may be a long process of regrets. Spend the time and money to make this decision the correct decision. You will never regret the amount spent, for high quality equipment and installation.

CHAPTER TEN

OUTBOARD ENGINES

The outboard engine has been popular in recreational boating for more than sixty years. The first outboards were one or two horsepower and weighed as much as a twenty horse engine of today. As the years progressed, the design concerns became directed towards smaller, lighter, faster and more efficient engines. The first outboard engine (Pictured below) to break the one hundred horsepower barrier, was built in 1962 by Mercury Marine. With this advancement, the engines have grown in size to the current three hundred horsepower engines.

Courtesy of Mercury Outboards

Another important advancement in outboard design, came to us from Honda. This manufacturer was the first to build a four cycle outboard engine. The next major turning point was the outboard diesel engine. It is becoming apparent the only industry pushing harder for <u>Smaller</u>, <u>Faster</u>, <u>Lighter</u> than the outboard engine manufactures, is the computer industry. With all of these advancements, the fact remains, the Lion's share of the industry belongs to the two cycle outboard engines.

The information in this chapter will be general to all two cycle outboards, ranging from two to twenty horse power. Although few of the basic operating functions change from the small two cycle outboards to the largest of engines, I will limit the information to the engines most commonly used on a tender.

There are several maintenance items, which if attended to regularly, will keep the outboard engine in good working order. These engines are designed and built to give years of trouble free service with a minimum of effort on the owner's part. However, failure to meet this minimum, will surely bring an early demise to even the best built engine. With the proper maintenance a good outboard can last more than thirty years.

My 1970, six horsepower Johnson, is living proof of this fact. It has been used as a fishing motor on john boats, tender motor and as a small sailboat kicker since its purchase by me. After all these years of hard use, it has never left me stranded. It is running as strong today as when it was new. I attribute this longevity to a well-built engine and my vigilance towards the engine's maintenance.

I suggest purchasing the shop manual for the outboard engines you own. This manual will supply the information needed to properly maintain and repair the engine. Following the steps in the shop manual and the advice below, will extend the life of your engine.

The first step for any outboard used in salt water, is the removal of the lower unit bolts. When the bolts are removed, coat the entire bolt with an anti-seize compound (Anti-seize compound is the best product to use.), gasket sealant or even petroleum jelly. This small step will help tremendously when the lower unit must be removed to replace the water pump or other internal components.

The steering shaft and possibly other components of the motor will have grease fittings. These fittings should be greased regularly, with a high quality marine grease incorporating Teflon®. If this is not accomplished, the steering or other areas will begin to stiffen. When this occurs it may entail a major repair to loosen the offending component.

There are several areas on most outboards which require lubrication using a spray lubricant with a long tube. W-D40®, with the spray tube attached, is an excellent choice for these areas. The areas are indicated by a stub of metal with a small hole in the center. The spray tube is placed into the hole and the lubricant is injected.

The lower unit of the outboard should be flushed with each use. This is often impractical if the engine is used on a tender, as it may rarely be near a fresh water hose. Under this circumstance, flush the engine with fresh water as often as possible.

The lower unit of an outboard motor can be flushed easily by using a pair of "ear muffs". This device, available at all marine stores, slips over the water intake screens of the lower unit. These screens are generally located forward of the prop, below the cavitation plate. After the muff is in place, a garden hose is connected and the water is turned on. Start the engine and allow it to idle for three to five minutes, to thoroughly flush the sea water from the engine's cooling system.

CAUTION: Hearing protection is suggested since an outboard engine is extremely loud, when the engine is out of the water.

One of the most important routine maintenance steps is checking and changing the lower unit oil regularly. Water penetration into the lower unit oil is not an uncommon occurrence. The water will degrade the oil and retard lubrication. Therefore, it is prudent to check the oil monthly and change it at the first sign of degradation. The oil should be changed every six months regardless of its state.

To check the lower unit oil you must have the engine in the down position and level. Remove the machine screw located slightly above the cavitation plate. If oil flows out or the oil is level with the hole, the oil level is sufficient. If oil is below the hole, or the oil is discolored, (light brown or white) the oil must be changed. If the oil is discolored, it would be wise to remove an oil sample and have a mechanic give their opinion on the cause of the discoloration. It may be water penetration or a much more severe situation. A trained eye will know at a glance.

To change the lower unit oil, simply remove the machine screw located in the lower unit forward and slightly lower than the center of the prop. Have a large coffee can under this opening to catch the waste oil. Next, remove the top screw, if you have reinstalled it after checking the oil level, and allow all the oil to drain from the lower unit.

Replace the oil with the proper lubricant as recommend by the manufacturer of the engine. This is easiest when you purchase a pump or use the quart size or larger container of oil, with a pointed tip. Insert the pump end or the tip, tightly into the lower screw hole. Pump in the oil or squeeze the bottle, until oil flows from the top hole. Replace the top machine screw first. Remove the pump or bottle and quickly install the lower machine screw.

Outboard engines built after the mid-seventies rarely have point sets. Engines built prior to that time will have one set of points for each cylinder. The newer engines will simply need the plugs changed regularly while the older models will also need the point sets changed.

A few steps should be taken to assure a professional quality tune up, both in performance and appearance. Attach the "ear muffs" and start the water flow. Warm the engine to one half operating temperature. When the engine has reached this temperature, spray carburetor cleaner into the carburetor. This will clean the fuel intake system of the engine. The same product can be used on the exterior of the carburetor to clean off any residue or grime. Allow the engine to idle until the exhaust is burning clean, at which time the engine should be shut down.

A clean engine has many advantages. It is easier to work on, easier to spot fluid leaks, it will run cooler and will appear professionally maintained. Still many people believe this simple step to be a waste of time. I do not agree in the least.

While the engine is still warm from cleaning the carburetor, use an engine cleaning product to remove all the grease, grime and general crust from the outside of the engine. Be certain the carburetor and distributor are well covered before you apply this product to the engine. Follow the manufacturer's directions for the application and removal of the products you have chosen.

After the engine has been cleaned and has had time to cool down, you can start the replacement of the different tune up components. I have a routine I use for every engine I tune. I stay with this routine time and time again. In doing so I find I do not forget any of the necessary steps. I will relay my tune up routine which you can then adjust to your liking, but don't skip any of the steps I have included. Refer to your shop manual for the correct gap settings for the plugs and point set.

Start by setting the gap of the new plugs, using a feeler gauge or a gapping tool. The gapping tool loosely resembles a pair of pliers and is designed to keep the gap constant across the tip of the plug. Working on only one of the cylinders at a time, disconnect the plug wire, remove the old plug, install the new plug and reattach the plug wire. By working on one cylinder at a time you do not run the risk of connecting the plug wire to the wrong spark plug.

After all of the spark plugs have been changed, remove the flywheel. This can be accomplished by removing the flywheel retaining nut in the center of the flywheel and using a flywheel puller. If this tool is not available, the use of two screwdrivers, one placed under opposite sides of the flywheel, can be used to pry up on the flywheel. As you pry up on the flywheel, tap the top of the shaft with a brass hammer. Be certain to partially install the flywheel retaining nut on the shaft threads. This step will protect them from damage by the hammer.

Replace the points, condenser and if necessary, the wires and coil. Remove and install only one component at a time. You may need an ignition wrench set and ignition screwdriver to complete this work. Be certain to use the small capsule of grease to lubricate the shaft cam lobes. (The part of the shaft on which the points ride.)

After the points are installed they will need to be adjusted. To accomplish this, the points must rest on the high side of the distributor shaft lobe. You can turn the engine, to get the points on the high side, by threading the nut onto the shaft and turning it with a socket and socket wrench. Be certain to turn the engine in the direction of its rotation.

When the points are resting at the proper location, slightly loosen the screw holding the points in place. Slide the proper size feeler gauge between the two contact points on the point set and tighten the screw. Remove and reinsert the feeler gauge. As you are doing this you should not see any movement in the contact points, but you should feel a slight resistance as you move the feeler gauge blade between the contact points. Tighten the screw and check the gap.

When all the components are properly installed and adjusted the flywheel can be installed. Tighten the fly wheel to the correct torque setting, as stated in the shop manual.

Replacing the water pump of an outboard engine, will be the most difficult of the maintenance jobs. This is often complicated by frozen bolts. If you encounter bolts which do not turn, Liquid Wrench® should be applied and allowed time to work. After an hour of soaking in Liquid Wrench®, tap the head of the bolt with a brass hammer. Next, turn the bolt slightly in the direction to tighten the bolt. This will help free the threads. Next, turn the bolts in the direction to loosen the bolts. If all of these steps fail, the bolts will shear off as they are being removed. If this is the case, you may have enough bolt remaining to lock Vise-Grips® in place and use the above steps to remove the bolts with the Vise-Grips®. If this step does not work, the only solution will be drilling out the remaining bolt and tapping new threads into the casing. This is a project best left to a professional, as damage can readily occur if the drill slips or the hole is drilled at the slightest angle.

When all the bolts are removed from the lower unit, refer to your shop manual for the correct sequence of steps involved, to complete the removal of the lower unit.

With the lower unit removed, the water pump impeller can be removed. This may entail the removal of a pin, bolt or screw through the impeller and shaft. When the water pump impeller has been removed, the shaft seal can be removed by prying it out of the seat.

Install the new seal in the same direction (same side down) as the old seal. Lubricate the seal and impeller well, using marine grease or petroleum jelly. Slide the new seal over the shaft with the correct side facing down. Lightly tap the seal into its seat, using a brass hammer and if necessary, a small block of wood. Install the water pump impeller exactly as it was removed.

The lower unit can now be installed on the engine. Be certain all the correct components have been properly seated, in the proper locations. Entirely coat all the bolts with an anti-seize thread compound to reduce corrosion and make future removal easier.

One concern many boaters overlook, when the tender is decommissioned for short periods of time, is the proper storage of the engine. This simple project will save hours of frustration when the engine is placed into service. These few steps should be taken when the engine will be out of service for three weeks or longer.

The first step is treating the fuel with a fuel stabilizer. When this is accomplished, start the engine with the ear muffs in place. Allow the engine to run for five minutes. Shut down the engine by disconnecting the fuel supply line and allowing the engine to run out of fuel. This will accomplish two phases of the storage process. The engine will have the cooling system flushed and the engine will be void of fuel in the fuel system.

The next step is to remove the spark plugs. Spray an engine fogger into the carburetor while pulling on the starting cord. Spray the same product into each cylinder. Using the starting cord, turn the engine one revolution and spray the fogger into the cylinders again. Replace the spark plugs. Spray the entire exterior of the engine's power head with the engine fogger. The fogging of the engine provides good protection from corrosion, both on the interior and exterior of the engine.

When the time arrives to place the engine into service, simply connect the fuel line and check the spark plugs and spark plug wires to be certain they are secure. Start the engine. The engine will run with smoky exhaust for the first few minutes of operation. As the fogging spray is burnt off, the exhaust should return to normal.

The small outboard engines, commonly used to power the ship's tender, are easy engines to maintain and repair. The longer you have the same engine, the more familiar you become with the workings of that engine. As time passes, you will feel comfortable tackling the in-depth projects the engine may require as it ages. As I stated earlier, maintenance is the key to an outboard engine's longevity. With a little care, these engines can last for years, without leaving you stranded at the dock.

APPENDIX ONE

TOOLS AND SUPPLIES TO CONSIDER OWNING

As you delve deeper into the work of owning a boat, you will always find a need for one more tool, or you should "stock" more supplies for the work. It is truly a case of "Too much is never enough, and enough is always too much". With this in mind it is best to adapt the following to your boat's needs, not your needs.

HAND TOOLS

Good brands are Craftsman, Snap On (both have a life time warranty), Channel Lock, Vaco, Greenlee, & Mac. I would not recommend any others, for I have not used them.
1, #2, #3 Phillips screwdrivers.
Thin blade 3/16", medium blade 1/4", heavy blade 3/8" straight screwdrivers.
All the above should also be purchased in the stubby length.
Jewelers set of screwdrivers.
Various square drivers if you have this type of fastener on your boat. You will have to know the sizes you will need.
Linesman pliers.
Dikes/side cutters.

Wire strippers. Buy the type with the stripper portion before
the hinge.
Terminal crimps.
Digital multi-meter.
Long nose pliers.
Needle nose pliers.
Vise Grips
Small slip joint pliers (opens to 2").
Straight blade sheet metal cutters.
Caulk gun.
Lufkin folding rule with brass slide extension.
Large and small metal files.
Set of allen wrenches 1/16" to 7/16" minimum.
China bristles paint brushes with an angle cut, in sizes 1",
1-1/2", 2", 2-1/2".
School pencils.
Pencil sharpener.
Thin blade awl.
8" & 12" adjustable wrench.
12" Lenox hacksaw with 18, 24, & 32 teeth per inch blades.
Estwing leather handle straight claw hammer.
A #2, & #3 nail set.
Combination wrench set.
1/4" drive socket set.
3/8" drive socket set.
Ignition wrench set.
I use the term "set" because most of these tools are sold in
sets. You can purchase them individually but you will
spent more than buying a set.
24" to 36" Adjustable wrench. The size will depend on the
prop nut size of your boat.
Battery carrying strap.
Feeler gauges (blade type).
Cordless drill with two batteries, charger, Cobalt drill bits
ranging from 1/32" to 3/8" and screwdriver bits with
a good holder. These should be the same size as your

hand screwdrivers.

Large slip joint pliers (opens to 4").

2# Ballpeen hammer.

Caulking iron.

Rubber mallet.

Small & large Wonder bars.

Diston small dovetail saw.

Diston coping saw.

Diston 13 point hand saw.

Stanley 25' tape measure.

Stanley combination square.

Stanley #40 wood chisels 1/2", 3/4", 1"

These are the only Stanley tools you should own.

Block plane.

Half round wood file/rasp.

Heavy blade awl.

Larger size drill bits 7/16" to 1" forsener bits are the best for large wood bits. Metal bits should be cobalt.

Brad point bits 1/16" to 3/8".

Plug cutters 3/8" to 3/4"

Hole saw set.

Metal chisel and drift set.

Right angle-straight and phillips screwdrivers.

Fish tape.

Heavy gauge terminal crimp tool.

Line wrench set.

1/2" drive socket set.

Deep well socket set for all the different size drives you now own. Some of these may have been included when you purchased the sets.

1/2 " Breaker bar.

1/2" Click stop torque wrench.

1/2" drive large sockets for all the bolts/nuts which are larger than the sets contain.

Wrenches for the same bolts/nuts.

POWER TOOLS

I only recommend these manufacturers, I have had great they last years under heavy use. You should be able to list these in your will with the confidence your children will still get many years of use from them. There is no reason to buy lesser quality power tools. They don't do the job as well or as quickly as these will. Makita, Industrial Grade Black & Decker, Delta, and Skil, Porter Cable, Freud, Bosch, Milwaukee (You will pay extra for the name "Milwaukee".)

3/8" & 1/2" power drills.

Circular saw with good carbide tooth blades.

Random orbiting sander (Porter Cable only) with 5" & 6" pads. Buy your 3M gold sanding disk in the 6" size, and cut them down when you need the 5" size. Buy rolls of these grits. 60, 80, 100, 120, 150, 180.

Power miter box with an 80 tooth carbide blade.

3" x 24" or 4" x 24" belt sander. Buy at least three belts of each of these grits. 36, 80, 100, 120.

Soldering gun with electrical solder and flux.

Heat gun.

Random orbit buffer if you own a fiberglass boat.

Scrolling jig saw with various wood and metal blades.

Router with various bits purchased as the jobs warrant. Always use roller bearing bits where applicable.

Sawz-all with various size and types of blades for wood/metal.

Biscuit jointer with at least two hundred of the two larger size biscuits.

25', 50', & 75' #12 wire extension cords.

Craftsman table or radial arm saw. These are both fair tools and can be purchased inexpensively when used. The radial arm saw can be set up with a multitude of attachments to handle many different functions other than cross cutting and ripping.

SUPPLIES

All Stainless Steel Fasteners

At least 50 each of these phillips head screws.

x 1/2", 3/4", 1" Flat and oval head.

#6 x 1/2", 3/4", 1", 1-1/4", 1-1/2", 1-3/4", 2" Flat and oval head.

#8, #10, #12 Same as #6 plus 2-1/2", 3" Flat and oval head.

Finish washers for each of the above size screw numbers.

#6, #8, #10, 1/2", 3/4", 1", 1-1/2" Pan head.

At least 10 each of these fasteners.

1/4" x 20 x 2", 3", 4" Flat and stove head bolts with 2 washers and 1 nut each.

5/16" & 3/8" x 1", 1-1/2", 2", 2-1/2", 3" machine bolts with 2 washers and 1 nut each.

Cap nuts for each of the above sizes.

1/4" x 2", 3", 4", 5" lag bolts with washers.

Large fender washers for each of the above sizes.

2 pieces of solid rod 3' long in 1/4", 3/8", 1/2".

2 pieces of threaded rod 3' long with 6 nuts and washers per piece in 1/4", 3/8", 1/2".

Various size cotter pins to replace ones which will need removed. Check the sizes you need before ordering or purchase a cotter pin kit with various sizes included.

18 gauge brass or stainless steel brads in 1/2", 3/4", 1"

Electrical

Butt terminals, male and female quick disconnect terminals. Order at least 50 each for wire gauges, 22-18, 16-14, 12-10, 8.

Spade connectors, stud connectors. Order at least 50 each for the same gauge of wire above to fit around stud sizes 4-6, 8-10, 1/4", 5/16", 3/8".

10 terminals for each size battery cable in use on your boat.

6 battery clamps (lugs, the kind used on your car) with stud. Do not connect the battery wires directly to the clamp; use the stud and terminals.

200 each of 6" & 11" medium duty wire ties.

100 each of 3/4" and 1-1/2" cable clamps.

1 each 4, 6, 8, 10 position terminal blocks. 6 each 20 amp in-line fuse holders with 5 each of, 5 amp, 10 amp, 15 amp, & 20 amp fuses.

100 ft each of wire gauges 18, 16, 14, 12, 10, 8. Tinned marine primary wire.

25 ft each of wire gauges 6, & 4.

10 butt connectors for 6 & 4 wire.

10 ft of battery cable for each size you have in use on board.

2 ft each of heat shrink tubing 3/16", 1/4", 3/8", 1/2," 3/4".

Misc. Electrical Supplies

Liquid electrical tape.

Vinyl electrical tape.

Nylon string to use as a wire fishing device.

1 Pair of battery jumper cables. They must be long enough to reach between the banks of batteries you may need to jump. If you can not find them this long, make up your own with heavy ends and # 2 battery cable.

Jumper wires for testing. These can be made with 4 alligator clips and 12 gauge wire.

1 breaker or fuse holder for each different size and type you on have board.

1 fuse for each specialty fuse on board.

1 switch for each type on board.

2 extra bulbs for each type on board.

1 lamp socket for each type on board.

1 of each shore line end or an extra 50' shore line set.

1 connector for each type of electronic instrument connector on board.

Sealants, Paint and Repair Products

1 tube each of Teak Deck Systems, 3M 5200 in white, GE silicone in white & clear, Star Bright polysulfide under water sealant, Sea Repair.

1 small kit each of Epoxy, Marine Tex, Boat Yard fiberglass with 6 oz. cloth and matching gel coat colors.

1 qt each of Ephifane varnish, Sekkens Cetol, InterLux top sides paint for each color on board, stain, Star Brite Tropical Teak oil and sealer, paint thinner, acetone, lacquer thinner, Penatrol, boiled linseed oil.

Coffee cans.

Plastic pots in 1 qt size.

Disposable brushes in 1/2", 1", 1-1/2", 2", 2-1/2".

Plumbing Parts

The best method of determining your needs for plumbing will be to go through your supply and waste systems measuring each hose, clamp, tubing and fitting type and size. With this list in hand purchase at least 2 of each type of fitting, 10 of each size clamp, hose to replace the longest length of each size or fittings and hose to patch in the very long lengths. As with your shore power line, carry an extra water supply hose of no less than 50'. Also purchase water hose repair ends.

This may not be considered plumping by some, but it carries water, therefore I will include it in this section. Your engines have many small sizes and lengths of hoses. As with the plumbing hoses, buy enough to replace the longest length of each size with the proper size clamps. These should be the heavy wall hose with wire reinforcement.

If you have large exhaust lines you do not need to carry a full length. Do carry a large coffee can with 4 hose clamps which are a larger size than to the exhaust hose. I will note at this time you must have at least 1 extra impeller for every impeller on board. THIS IS A MUST!

Misc. Supplies

Shock cords and ends.
Buckets.
Sponges.
Chamois.
Toilet brush.
Scrub brush.
Deck brush with handle.
Roller handle, pan and pads.
Bronze wool.
Bronze scrub brush.
Detergents.
Cleaning products.
Polishes.
Compounds.
Water resistant/proof glue.
Extension cord ends.
Dinghy patch material. (Patch kit for every inflatable on board.)
Repair parts for engine(s).
Antifreeze.
Oils.
Grease gun with grease.
Transmission fluid.
5 gals of extra fuel.
Duct tape.
Riggers tape.
Masking tape.
Sheet sand paper in grits 50, 80, 100, 120, 150, 180, 220. At least 5 sheets of each grit.
At least two complete sets of dock lines and anchor rodes.
One 3/4" line (regardless of boat size to 45') three times the length of the boat. (Tow line)

Anything else you would not feel comfortable leaving home or the dock without having on board.

APPENDIX TWO

SUPPLIERS AND MANUFACTURERS

The following list of Suppliers and Manufacturers in no way constitutes a complete directory of all the fine manufacturers and suppliers available throughout the country. I listed the companies I dealt with in the past and that I am comfortable recommending to my fellow boaters. This in no way means you should only deal with these companies; as always ask your friends for their recommendations. In most cases you will not be disappointed following their guidance.

Suppliers

Boat/US: Boat Supplies 1-800-937-2628 880 S Pickett St. Alexandria, VA   22304

Defender: Boat Supplies 1-800-628-8225 P. O. Box 820 New Rochelle, NY   10802-0820

Diesel Engineering & Marine Services: Engine repair and parts, 1-800-742-1169, P O Box 276, Port Salerno, FL   34992

Depco Pump Co: Pump supplies and parts, 813-446-1656, 1227 S Linoln Ave., Clearwater FL   34616

E & B Discount Marine: Boat Supplies 1-800-262-8464 P O Box 3138 Edison, NJ   08818-3138

Home Depot: Tools/Supplies Located in most cities throughout the country. Look for them in your local phone
books.
Jamestown Distributors: Boat Building/Repairing Supplies
1-800-423-0030 28 Narragansett Ave. P O Box 348
Jamestown, RI 02835
Marine Propulsion: Genset & transmission repair, 561-283-
6486, 3201 S. E. Railroad Ave., Stuart, FL 34997
West Marine: Boat Supplies, 1-800-538-0775, P O Box
50050, Watsonville, CA 95077-5050

Manufacturers

Alaska Diesel Electric: Engines, 206-789-3880, 4420 14
Ave. N. W., Seattle, WA 98107-0543
Balmar: Alternators and Controls, 902 NW Ballard Way,
Seattle, WA 98107
Caterpillar: Engines, 800-447-4986, 2001 Ruppman Plaza,
Peoria, IL 61614
Cummings Marine: Engines, 803-745-1171, 4500 Leeds
Ave., Suite 301, Charleston, SC 29405
Datamarine International, Inc.: Electronics Instruments,
508-563-7151, 53 Portside Drive, Pocasset, MA
02559
Davis Instruments: Navigation instruments, 415-732-9229,
3465 Diablo Ave., Hayward, CA 94545
Daytona Marine Engine Corp.: Engines, 904-676-1140, 1815
North U. S. 1, Ormond Beach, FL 32174
Detroit Diesel: Engines, 313-592-5000, 13400 Outer Drive
West, Detroit, MI 48239
Deutz MWM/KHD Canada: Engines, 514-335-3150, 4420
Garand, Ville St. Laurent, Quebec, Canada H4R 2A3
Espar Heater Systems: Cabin Heaters, 416-670-0960, 6435
Kestrel Road, Mississauga, Ontario, Canada L5T
128
Fireboy Halon Systems Division-Convenience Marine

Products, Inc.: Fire suppression equipment, 616-454-8337, P O Box 152, Grand Rapids, MI 49501

Furuno USA Inc.: Electronics, 415-873-4421, P O Box 2343, South San Fransico, CA 94083

Galley Maid Marine Products, Inc.: Galley, Water supply and waste, 407-848-8696, 4348 Westroads Drive, West Palm Beach, FL 33407

Heart Interface Corp.: Inverters, Chargers, Monitors, Electrical 1-800-446-6180, 21440 68th Ave. South, Kent, WA 98032

Hubbell Wiring Device Division, Hubbell Inc.: Electrical products, 203-337-3348, P O Box 3999, Bridgeport, CT 06605

Icom America, Inc.: Electronics, 206-454-8155, 2380-116th Ave. NE, Bellevue, WA 98004

Interlux Paints: Varnish, Paint, Coatings, 908-964-2285, 2270 Morris Ave, Union, NJ 07083

Lister-Petter, Ltd: Engines, 913-764-3512, 815 East 56 Highway, Olathe, KS 66061

MAN Marine Engines: Engines, 954-771-9092, 6555 N. W. 9 Ave., Suite 306, Ft. Lauderdale, FL 33309

Marinco Electrical Products: Electrical products, 415-883-3347, One Digital Drive, Novato, CA 94949

MerCruiser: Engines, 405-743-6704, Stillwater, OK 74075

Marine Corporation Of America: Engines, 317-738-9408, 980 Hurricane Road, Franklin, IN 46131

Micrologic: Electronics, 818-998-1216, 20801 Dearborn Street, Chatsworth, CA 91311

New England Ropes, Inc.: All types of line, 508-999-2351, Popes Island, New Bedford, MA 02740

Onan: Gensets, 612-574-5000, 1400 73rd Ave. NE, Minneapolis, MN 55432

Paneltronics: Electrical panels, 305-823-9777, 11960 NW 80th CT, Hialeah Gardens, FL 33016

Powerline: Alternators and controls, 1-800-443-9394, 4616 Fairlane Ave, Ft Worth, TX 76119

Racor Division-Parker Hannifin Corporation: Fuel filters, 800-344-3286, P O Box 3208, Modesto, CA 95353

Raritan Engineering Company, Inc.: Heads, Treatment systems, Charging systems, 609-825-4900

Ray Jefferson Company: Electronics, 215-487-2800, Main & Cotton Sts., Philadelphia, PA 19127

Raytheon Marine Company: Electronics, 603-881-5200, 46 River Road, Hudson, NH 03051

Resolution Mapping: Electronic charts and software 617-860-0430, 35 Hartwell Ave. Lexington, MA 02173

Sea Recovery Corporation: Water purification, 213-327-4000, P O Box 2560, Gardena, CA 90247

Seagull Water Purification Systems: Water purification, 203-384-9335, P O Box 271, Trumbull, CT 06611

Star Brite: Coatings /Sealants 1-305-587-6280, 4041 S W 47th Ave Ft. Lauderdale, FL 33314

Statpower Technologies Corp: Chargers, Inverters, 7725 Lougheed Hwy, Burnby, BC Canada V5A 4V8

Teak Deck Systems Teak deck caulking 813-377-4100, 6050 Palmer Blvd. Sarasota, FL 34232

The Guest Company, Inc.: Electrical components, Chargers, Inverters, 203-238-0550, P O Box 2059 Station A, Meriden, CT 06450

Trace Engineering: Chargers, Inverters, 206-435-8826, 5917-195th NE, Arlington, WA 98223

Vanner Weldon Inc. Inverters & Chargers, 614-771-2718, 4282 Reynolds Dr. Hilliard, Ohio 43026-1297

Webasto Heater, Inc.: Cabin Heaters, 313-545-8770, 1458 East Lincoln, Madison Hts, MI 48071

Westerbeke: Engines, 617-588-7700, Avon Industrial Park, Avon, MA 02322

West System Epoxy: Gougeon Brothers, Inc., 517-684-7286, P. O. Box 908, Bay City, MI 48707

Woolsey / Z-Spar: Paint, Varnish, Coatings, 800-221-4466, 36 Pine St, Rockaway, NJ 07866

Yanmar Diesel America Corp.: Engines, 708-541-1900, 901 Corporate Drive, Buffalo Grove, IL 60089-4508

GLOSSARY

In this glossary, I have tried to give you some of the most common terms used in boating and on boats. It is not intended to cover the many thousands of words and terms contained in the language exclusive to boating. The longer you are around boats and boaters the more of this second language you will learn. You will also find this language holds little value on land.

A

Accumulator tank-A tank used to add air pressure to the fresh water system thus reducing water pump run time.

Aft-Near the stern.

Amidships-Midway between the bow and stern.

Antifouling-Bottom paint used to prevent growth on the bottom of boats.

Athwartships-Any line running at a right angle to the fore/aft centerline of the boat.

B

Backer plate-Metal plate used to increase the strength of a through bolt application, such as with the installation of a cleat.

Ballast-Weight added to improve sea handling abilities of the
boat or to counter balance an unevenly loaded boat.
Beam-The width of the boat at it's widest point.
Bilge- The lowest point inside a boat.
Bilge pump-Underwater water pump used to remove water
from the bilge.
Binnacle-A box or stand used to hold the compass.
Bolt-Any fastener with any head style and machine thread
shank.
Boot stripe-Trim paint of a contrasting color located just
above the bottom paint on the hull sides.
Breaker-Replaces a fuse to interrupt power on a given
electrical circuit when that circuit becomes
overloaded or shorted.
Bridge-The steering station of a boat.
Brightwork-Polished metal or varnished wood aboard a boat.
Bristol Fashion-The highest standard of condition any vessel
can obtain and the highest state of crew seamanship.
The publishing company which brought you this
book.
Bulkhead-A wall running across (athwartships) the boat.
Butt connectors-A type of crimp connector used to join two
wires end to end in a continuing run of the wire.

C

Canvas-A general term used to describe cloth material used
for boat coverings of any type. A type of cloth
material.
Cavitation-Turbulance caused by prop rotation which
reduces the efficiency of the prop.
Chafing gear-Any material used to prevent the abrasion of
another material.
Chain locker-A forward area of the vessel used for chain
storage.
Chain-Equally sized inter-looping oblong rings commonly

used for anchor rode.

Chine-The turn of the hull below the waterline on each side of the boat. A sailboat hull, displacement hull and semi-displacement hull all have a round chine. Planing hulls all have a hard (sharp corner) chine.

Chock-A metal fitting used in mooring or rigging to control the turn of the lines.

Cleat-A device used to secure a line aboard a vessel or on a dock.

Coaming-A barrier around the cockpit of a vessel to prevent water from washing into the cockpit.

Cockpit-Usually refers to the steering area of a sailboat or the fishing area of a sport fishing boat. The sole of this area is always lower than the deck.

Companionway-An entrance into a boat or a stairway from one level of a boat's interior to another.

Cribbing-Large blocks of wood used to support the boat's hull during it's time on land.

Cutlass Bearing-A rubber "tube" inserted into a strut in which the shaft rides.

D

Davit-Generally used to describe a lifting device for a dinghy.

Delaminate-A term used to discribe two or more layers of any adhered material seperated from each other.

Device-A term used in conjunction with electrical systems. Generally used to describe lights, switches, and receptacles, etc.

Dinghy-Small boat used as a tender to the mother ship.

Displacement hull-A boat supported by its own ability to float while underway.

Displacement-The amount of water, in weight, displaced by the boat when floating.

Dock-Any land based structure used for mooring a boat.

Draft-The amount of space (water) a boat needs between its waterline and the bottom of the body of water. When a boat's draft is greater than the water depth, you are aground.

Dry rot-This is not a true term as the decay of wood actually occurs in moist conditions.

F

Fairing compound-The material used to achieve the fairing process.

Fairing-The process of smoothing a portion of the boat so it will present a very even and smooth surface after the finish is applied.

Fairlead-A portion of rigging used to turn a line, cable or chain to increase the radius of the turn and thereby reduce friction.

Fall-The portion of a block and tackle system that moves up or down.

Fastening-Generally used to describe a means by which the planking is attached to the structure of the boat. Also used to describe screws, rivets, bolts, nails etc. (fastener)

Fiberglass-Cloth like material made from glass fibers and used with resin and hardener to increase the resin strength.

Filter-Any device used to filter impurities from any liquid or air.

Fin keel-A recent type of keel design. Resembles an up-side-down T when viewed from fore or aft.

Flame arrestor -A safety device placed on top of a gasoline carburetor to stop the flame flash of a backfiring engine.

Flat head-A screw head style which can be made flush with or recessed into the wood surface.

Float switch-An electrical switch commonly used to

automatically control the on-off of a bilge pump. When this device is used, the pump is considered to be an automatic bilge pump.

Flying bridge-A steering station high above the deck level of the boat.

Fore-and-aft-A line running parallel to the keel. The keel runs fore-and-aft.

Fore-The front of a boat.

Forecastle-The area below decks in the forward most section of the boat. (pronunciation is often fo'c's'le)

Foredeck-The front deck of a boat.

Forward-Any position in front of amidships.

Freeboard-The distance on the hull from the waterline to the deck level.

Full keel-A long used keel design with heavy lead ballast and deep draft. This keel runs from the stem, to the stern at the rudder.

G

Galley-The kitchen of a boat.

Gelcoat-The outer-most laminate of the fiberglass lamination that provides the shine and smooth finish.

Gimbals-A method of supporting anything which must remain level regardless of the boat's attitude.

Grommet-A ring pressed into a piece of cloth through which a line can be run.

Gross tonnage-The total interior space of a boat.

Ground tackle-Refers to the anchor, chain, line and connections as one unit.

H

Hanging locker-A closet with a rod for hanging clothes.

Hatch-A opening with a lid which openings in an upward direction.

Hauling-Removing the boat from the water. The act of pulling on a line or rode is also called hauling.

Hawsehole-A hull opening for mooring lines or anchor rodes.

Hawsepipes-A pipe through the hull, for mooring or anchor rodes.

Head-The toilet on a boat. Also refers to the entire area of the bathroom on a boat.

Helm-The steering station and steering gear.

Holding tank-Used to hold waste for disposal ashore.

Hose-Any flexible tube capable of carrying a liquid.

Hull-The structure of a vessel not including any component other than the shell.

I

Inboard-Positioned towards the center of the boat. An engine mounted inside the boat.

K

Keel-A downward protrusion running fore and aft on the center line of any boat's bottom. It is the main structural member of a boat.

King plank-The plank on the center line of a wooden laid deck.

Knees-A structural member reinforcing and connecting two other structural members.

L

Launch-To put a boat in the water.

Lazarette-A storage compartment in the stern of a boat.

Limber holes-Holes in the bilge timbers of a boat to allow water to run to the lowest part of the bilge where it can be pumped out.

LOA-Length Over All. The over all length of a boat.

Locker-A storage area.

Log-A tube or cylinder through which a shaft or rudder stock runs from the inside of the boat to the outside of the boat. The log will have a packing gland (stuffing box) on the inside of the boat. Speed log is used to measure distance traveled. A book used to keep record of the events on board a boat.

LWL-Length On The Waterline. The length of a boat at the water line.

M

Marine gear-The term used for a boat's transmission.

Mast-An upward pointing timber used as the sail's main support. Also used on power and sail boats to mount flags, antennas, and lights.

Mile-A statute mile (land mile) is 5280 feet. A nautical mile (water mile) or knot is 6076.12 feet.

Mizzen mast- The aftermost mast on a sailboat.

N

Nautical mile-Equals 6076.12 feet.

Navigation lights-Lights required to be in operation while underway at night. The lighting pattern varies with the type, size and use of the vessel.

Nut-A threaded six sided device used in conjunction with a bolt.

Nylon-A material used for lines when some give is desirable. Hard nylon is used for some plumbing and rigging fittings.

O

Oval head-A screw head design used when the head can only

be partially recessed. The raised (oval) portion of the head will remain above the surface.

P

Painter-A line used to tow or secure a small boat or dinghy.

Pan head-A screw head design with a flat surface, used when the head will remain completely above the surface.

Panel-A term used to describe the main electrical distribution point, usually containing the breakers or fuses.

Pier-Same general usage as a dock.

Pile-A concrete or wooden post driven or otherwise embedded into the water's bottom.

Piling-A multiple structure of piles.

Pipe-A rigid, thick walled tube.

Planing hull-A hull design, which under sufficient speed, will rise above it's dead in the water position and seem to ride on the water.

Planking-The covering members of a wooden structure.

Plug-A term used to describe a pipe, tubing, or hose fitting. Describes any device used to stop water from entering the boat through the hull. A cylindrical piece of wood placed in a screw hole to "hide" the head of the screw.

Port-A land area for landing a boat. The left side of the boat when facing forward.

Propeller (Prop, Wheel, Screw)-Located at the end of the shaft. The prop must have at least two blades and propels the vessel through the water with a screwing motion.

R

Radar-A electronic instrument which can be used to "see" objects as "blips" on a display screen.

Rail-A non structural, safety member, on deck used as a

banister to help prevent falling overboard.

Ribs-Another term for frames. The planking is fastened to these structural members.

Rigging-Generally refers to any item placed on the boat after the delivery of the vessel from the manufacturer. Also refers to all the wire rope, line, blocks, falls, and other hardware needed for sail control.

Ring terminals-A crimp connector with a ring which can have a screw placed inside the ring for a secure connection.

Rode-Anchor line or chain.

Rope-Is a term which refers to cordage and this term is only used on land. When any piece of cordage is on board a boat it is referred to as line or one of it's more designating descriptions.

Round head-A screw or bolt head design with a round surface which remains completely above the material being fastened.

Rudder stock-Also known as rudder post. A piece of round, solid metal attached to the rudder at one end and the steering quadrant at the other.

Rudder-Located directly behind the prop and is used to control the steering of the boat.

S

Samson post-A large piece of material extending from the keel upward through the deck and is used to secure lines for mooring or anchoring.

Screw thread-A loosely spaced course thread used for wood and sheet metal screws.

Screw-A threaded fastener. A term for propeller.

Sea cock-A valve used to control the flow of water from the sea to the device it is supplying.

Shackle-A metal link with a pin to close the opening. Commonly used to secure the anchor to the rode.

Shaft-A solid metal cylinder which runs from the marine
gear to the prop. The prop is mounted on the end of
the shaft.

Shear pin-A small metal pin which is inserted through the
shaft and the propeller on small boats. If the prop hits
a hard object the shear pin will "shear" without
causing severe damage to the shaft.

Sheaves-The rolling wheel in a pulley.

Sheet metal screw-Any fastener which has a fully threaded
shank of wood screw threads.

Ship-Any seagoing vessel. To ship an item on a boat means
to bring it aboard.

Shock cord-An elastic line used to dampen the shock stress
of a load.

Slip-A docking space for a boat. A berth.

Sole-The cabin and cockpit floor.

Stanchion-A metal post which holds the lifelines or railing
along the deck's edge.

Starboard-The right side of the boat when facing forward.

Statute mile-A land mile which is 5280 feet.

Stem-The forward most structural member of the hull.

Step-The base of the mast where the mast is let into the keel
or mounted on the keel in a plate assembly.

Stern-The back of the boat.

Strut-A metal supporting device for the shaft.

Stuffing box-The interior end of the log where packing is
inserted to prevent water intrusion from the shaft or
rudder stock.

Surveyor-A person who inspects the boat for integrity and
safety.

Switch-Any device, except breakers, which interrupt the flow
of electrical current to a usage device.

T

Tachometer-A instrument used to count the revolutions of

anything turning, usually the engine, marine gear or shaft.

Tack rag-A rag with a sticky surface used to remove dust before applying a finish to any surface.

Tank-Any container of size that holds a liquid.

Tapered plug-A wooden dowel tapered to a blunt point and is inserted into a seacock or hole in the hull in an emergency.

Tender-A term used to describe a small boat (dinghy) used to travel between shore and the mother ship.

Terminal lugs-Car style, battery cable ends.

Through hull (Thru hull)-Any fitting between the sea and the boat which goes "through" the hull material.

Tinned wire-Stranded copper wire with a tin additive to prevent corrosion.

Topsides-Refers to being on deck. The part of the boat above the waterline.

Transmission-Refers to a marine or reduction gear.

Transom-The flat part of the stern.

Trim-The attitude with which the vessel floats or moves through the water.

Trip line-A small line made fast to the crown of the anchor. When weighing anchor this line is pulled to back the anchor out and thus release the anchor's hold in the bottom.

Tubing-A thin walled cylinder of metal or plastic, similar to pipe but having thinner walls.

Turn of the bilge-A term used to refer to the "corner" of the hull where the vertical hull sides meet the horizontal hull bottom.

V

Valves-Any device which controls the flow of a liquid.

Vessel-A boat or ship.

VHF radio-The electronic radio used for short range (10 to

20 mile maximum range) communications between shore and vessels and between vessels.

W

Wake-The movement of water as a result of a vessel's movement through the water.

Washer-A flat, round piece of metal with a hole in the center. A washer is used to increase the holding power of a bolt and nut by distributing the stress over a larger area.

Waste pump-Any device used to pump waste.

Water pump-Any device used to pump water.

Waterline-The line created at the intersection of the vessel's hull and the water's surface.

Wheel-Another term for prop, or the steering wheel of the boat.

Whipping-Refers to any method used, except a knot, to prevent a line end from unraveling.

Winch-A device used to pull in or let out line or rode. It is used to decrease the physical exertion needed to do the same task by hand.

Windlass-A type of winch used strictly with anchor rode.

Woodscrew-A fastener with only two thirds of the shank threaded with a screw thread.

Y

Yacht-A term used to describe a pleasure boat of some size. Usually used to impress someone.

Yard-A place where boats are stored and repaired.

Z

Zebra Mussel-A small fresh water mussel which will clog anything in a short period of time.

INDEX

A

Alcohol - 36, 37

B

Belts - 85

C

Condenser - 24, 104

D

Diesel - 1-4, 7, 9, 11, 17, 18, 21, 29, 30, 33-41, 44, 45, 52, 56, 60, 61, 87, 91, 94, 100
Distributor - 23-26, 103, 104

E

Exhaust - 13, 14, 19, 23, 47, 48, 53, 60-65, 91-96, 103, 106
Expansion Tank - 9, 10, 26, 27

F

Fuel & Fuel filters - 2-4, 7-46, 61, 78, 80, 90, 94, 96, 103, 106

G

Gasoline - 11, 17-19, 29-46, 60, 61, 87, 90, 91, 94
Genset - 93

H

Heat exchanger - 9, 10, 26, 27, 47, 48, 50, 53, 54

I

Injector - 11-16, 61, 62
Intake manifold - 23

M

Marine gear - 67

O

Oil - 4-9, 12, 18-22, 26, 30, 37, 53, 54, 61, 62, 70, 78, 80, 89, 94, 95, 101, 102
Oil cooler - 53, 54

P

Points - 24, 25, 29, 33, 41, 77, 89, 102, 104
Pulley - 24, 25, 84-86

R

Riser - 60-62

S

Spark plug - 11, 24, 26, 62, 103, 106

T

Through hull - 48, 53, 54, 89
Transmission - 53, 54, 67-74

V

Valves - 13-16, 44, 45, 50, 51

W

Water pump - 53, 56, 60, 95, 101, 104, 105

Books published by
Bristol Fashion Publications
Free catalog, phone 1-800-478-7147

Boat Repair Made Easy — Haul Out
Written By John P. Kaufman

Boat Repair Made Easy — Finishes
Written By John P. Kaufman

Boat Repair Made Easy — Systems
Written By John P. Kaufman

Boat Repair Made Easy — Engines
Written By John P. Kaufman

Standard Ship's Log
Designed By John P. Kaufman

Large Ship's Log
Designed By John P. Kaufman

Custom Ship's Log
Designed By John P. Kaufman

Designing Power & Sail
Written By Arthur Edmunds

Fiberglass Boat Survey
Written By Arthur Edmunds

Building A Fiberglass Boat
Written By Arthur Edmunds

Buying A Great Boat
Written By Arthur Edmunds

Outfitting & Organizing Your Boat For A Day, A Week or A Lifetime
Written By Michael L. Frankel

Boater's Book of Nautical Terms
Written By David S. Yetman

Modern Boatworks
Written By David S. Yetman

Practical Seamanship
Written By David S. Yetman

Captain Jack's Basic Navigation
Written By Jack I. Davis

Captain Jack's Celestial Navigation
Written By Jack I. Davis

Captain Jack's Complete Navigation
Written By Jack I. Davis

Southwinds Gourmet
Written By Susan Garrett Mason

The Cruising Sailor
Written By Tom Dove

Building A Fiberglass Boat
Written By Arthur Edmunds

Daddy & I Go Boating
Written By Ken Kreisler

Boat Repair Made Easy -- Engines, By John P. Kaufman

Complete Guide To Diesel Marine Engines
Written By John Fleming

Trouble Shooting Gasoline Marine Engines
Written By John Fleming

Whit   **ss**